From … Yours

Poems of Faith & Courage

By Marjorie Hundley Todd

From My Heart To Yours

Poems of Faith and Courage

By Marjorie Hundley Todd

ISBN: 978-1-934447-18-5

Published by,
Whispering Pines Publishing
11013 Country Pines Road
Shoals, IN 47581

Printed by,
Country Pines, Inc.
USA

Introduction:

From My Heart to Yours is a collections of poems gathered over the years from the life experiences of the author. Some were born in times of joy and gladness, and some were wrenched from the heart when sorrow could not be spoken. All came into being in times of communion with our Lord and Savior, Jesus Christ.

My prayer is that you will find encouragement from these simple words sent *From My Heart to Yours.*

Marjorie Todd

TABLE OF CONTENTS

Nature

The heavens declare the glory of God;
and the firmament showeth His handiwork.

Romans 1:20

The Land of Poetry

Poetry is a wonderful thing,
A world all its own.
It takes one out to the great beyond,
Into the vast unknown.
Poetry will take you beyond the moon,
And while you sit still in your chair,
You can visit the world of yesterday
And talk with the birds in the air.

You can fly on and on through the heavens,
Like a graceful cooing dove,
Walk all around on the Milky Way
And dance with the stars above.
You can sail to the sky on a rocket ship
While you lie still in bed,
Play hide and seek with the silver clouds
That dance about your head.

You can ride on the thunder up above,
And the raindrops all around
Will seem like diamonds in the air
As they travel to the ground.
You can deck your hair with the lightning,
From the snow flakes make a gown,
Make silver shoes from the sleet and hail
That's falling all around.

You can ride on a magic carpet
To the palace of a king,
Or sail right up to heaven
And hear the angels sing.
You can sink to the bottom of the ocean
On a ship within your mind,
Search and search through the regions there
And hidden treasures find.

You can drift, if you want, to the fountain of youth,
Drink from its crystal flow,
Be as young as you want to be,
And go where you want to go.
Yes, poetry is a wonderful thing,
And I just wish, don't you,
We all could live in the land of poems,
Where all our dreams come true.

A Poem For The Professor

"Don't be sentimental," you said,
"And don't use clichés, like break of dawn,
Windows of the mind, or a melody of spring.
Don't say winter wind or summer sun,
And please don't make rhyme;
Not in this day and time.
You must find another way to convey
What you want to say."
So I stopped being sentimental.
But when I crossed out the clichés
And erased the rhyme,
I was left with just a shell;
Then I found new words to describe
The silver streaks of light
Slowly smothering the dark
And the shimmering green of virgin buds
Clinging to drab brown limbs,
Awaiting a kiss from the golden orb of fire.
I saw new imagery for the frozen white
That rocks the world to sleep in its cradle of ice.
And when I filled in the blank spaces,
I had created a poem.

God's Flower

Man made a flower, a lovely flower
All velvety and fine,
With petals fair and pretty leaves
Around the stem entwined.
It looked as real as the fairest rose;
A thing of beauty rare.
Man made a flower, but he could not put
The flower's sweet fragrance there.

God made a flower, a lovely flower,
All velvety and fine,
With petals fair and pretty leaves
Around its stem entwined.
God made a flower, a lovely flower
A thing of beauty rare.
The sweetest perfume from it flows.
God put the fragrance there.

A Gentle Soothing Breeze

No artificial breeze is this
That blows its soothing balm,
Like gentle fingers touch a brow,
A troubled heart to calm.

No human hand could ere produce
This gentle, soothing breeze.
Must be the hand of God in love
That gently sways the trees.

Man can paint a picture
Of flowers and grass and sky,
Of clouds that lazily drift along
And birds that flutter by.

A scene of breathless beauty
Of a balmy autumn day,
With leaves of gold and brown and red
That fall along the way.

But man can't put the fragrance
In the flowers along the way.
Man can't paint the clean fresh smell
Of a field of new mown hay.

Man can't paint the cheerful song
The birds sing in the trees,
And man can never paint the touch
Of a gentle soothing breeze.

The Tree

I see her from my kitchen window,
A huge silhouette against the gray sky.
Her roots, gnarled and twisted
Push out from the ground like hands.
They grip the cover of snow in winter
And cause bare, brown patches
On the spread of green in summer.
It is true that in spring,
When her leaves are only tiny buds,
She is a promise of warmer days,
And in summer, the gift of green
She bears in her arms
Forms a canopy over my head.
But she opens her heart to the birds,
Holding their nests high
And sheltering their young.
They drop drippings on my car,
My patio and me. They are also noisy.
I once thought they were happy,
For they would awaken me early
With peeps and chirps.
Now I know they are fussing.
I hear them squabble and complain,
Yelling at each other in bird language.
And all the while
Their young are crying for something to eat.
I am grateful for the cool breeze she gives
And for her gift of shade.
But she guards my kitchen window
Like a jealous lover,
Refusing to let the sunshine in.
She throws twigs all over my yard,
And I have to pick them up
Before I can mow.

Her ugly old roots are eating up the soil
And working their way slowly
Into the sewer line.
Her branches, like a thousand arms,
Entangle themselves in the power line,
Clinging stubbornly, shaking the wires
With every gust of wind.
In autumn, she dresses herself in splashes of color
That change my yard
Into a world of splendor.
I love her then, when the air is crisp and cool,
And she send out a spray of perfume
That fills me with memories of childhood.
But even as I admire her, she shakes her head
And scatters leaves on the ground
And in the gutters of my house.
She stands defiantly
As I rake up her discarded mess
And stuff it into bags.
She seems pleased with herself
For all the trouble she causes.
She has grown crabby with age
And wants to dominate my yard
And control my life.
Someday a strong wind will blow her over,
Or lightning will strike her,
And she will fall,
Destroying everything in her path.
And I will miss her then.

Autumn

Cold dark clouds drift across the sky,
Crying tiny teardrops
That fall upon the earth.

Leaves, brown and orange, falling all around.
Playfully they dance
In happy joyful mirth.

Stately trees, standing straight and tall,
Patches of bright color
Against the blue sky.

Flickering flames, scent of burning wood,
Warmth from the fireplace
As evening draws nigh.

Glorious autumn! My heart reaches out
To hold it close
And keep it there forever.

I See The Stars

In the dark, it's hard to see
The path that lies ahead for me.
The sky above has lost its blue.
It's filled instead with darker hue,
And all around me lingers there
An awesome feeling of despair,
Doubts and fears and many scars.
But in the dark, I see the stars.

The tiny lights that flicker there
Appear as diamonds, sparkling rare.
They cast a steady stream of light
Like candles shining in the night.
I lift my eyes to God above,
And somehow know that He is love.
No darkness then, His goodness mars,
When in the dark, I see the stars.

My Weeping Willow Tree

The weeping willow tree in my front yard
Had long branches like angel wings
Brushing the ground.
When I pushed aside those graceful boughs,
I entered a world of magic.
My heart opened up
And drenching tears washed out
The loneliness, pain, sorrow,
And the feeling of always searching.
Answers to questions not yet asked
Surfaced beneath that tree.
I sat for hours on the cool ground,
Feeling safe and protected.
I could see bits of blue sky
Through the green dome of leaves
And feel the quiet stillness
Shut away from the noises of the world,
There I reached out to God
And felt His love reach out to me.

Four Seasons

I like the frozen wonder
When cold is all around,
And snowflakes, white and dazzling
Fall softly to the ground.
The world, a magic fairyland
In sparkling white is dressed,
Bringing peace and calm and stillness
That fills my heart with rest.

I like the budding springtime
When all around is seen
Peeping through the deadness
Little bits of green;
When raindrops softly falling,
With sweetness fills the air,
And tiny flowers of springtime
Are blooming everywhere.

I like the warmth of summer,
When days are hot and long,
And fireflies at evening
Dance to the cricket's song.
When night time's filled with wonder,
There's music everywhere,
And the sound of life and laughter
Flows out upon the air.

But oh! I love the autumn,
A magic color-land,
A wondrous burst of glory
Flung out by God's own hand.
I breathe the pungent fragrance
When the leaves begin to fall,
And my heart is filled with rapture
At the wonder of it all.

God's Light

When it's dark, I see the moon;
A great silver light sending out its rays,
Piercing the darkness,
Making the dark clouds glow,
Shining on my pathway
So that I can see the rough places.
Like the finger print of God,
It illuminates only what I should see.
I walk one step at a time,
Careful not to stray
From the circle of God's light.

Rain

I wouldn't like live where it does not rain,
Silently falling on field and plain.
There's something about refreshing showers
That enhances the fragrance of newborn flowers.
It makes the streets to shine like new,
And causes the rose buds, kissed with dew,
To burst forth in blossoms of vibrant hue.
The air is filled with the sweet perfume
Of grass washed clean and flowers in bloom,
And the earth is filled with the sound of rain
Playing a melody on my window pane.

Dawn

What light is this that slowly creeps
Its fingers all aglow,
Reaching for the darkness
That hovers o'er my soul?

I awakened in the stillness,
My heart bowed down with care.
Then I saw it pierce the shadows
And filter everywhere.

At first it entered slowly;
Just a tiny gleam of light,
But even as I watched,
It swallowed up the night,

And became a glorious sunrise
That lighted up the skies;
A vibrant burst of color
Before my very eyes.

My heart bowed to its beauty.
I breathed a silent prayer
For God who paints the sunrise
To brush away my care.

God's World

I woke up this morning to golden sunshine.
The skies over-head were so blue.
A cool breeze was blowing
O'er quiet waters flowing.
Lord I love this world made by you.

I love early mornings and quiet peaceful walks.
I love all the flowers by the way.
I love church bells ringing
And birds sweetly singing.
I thank God for His blessings each day.

The deserts, the valleys, the hills and the shore,
How glorious they are to behold.
The oceans, the fountains,
The rivers, the mountains
Their beauty has captured my soul.

The sunrise of life is fast fading away.
The sunset is coming out there.
My heart's filled with wonder.
I can see over yonder
My home He has gone to prepare.

This world can't compare with the beauty up there
In that city of unending day.
I'm anticipating
My Savior is waiting
When I come to the end of life's way.

Life

Life is indeed a great mystery
That rushes on day by day,
Like the dew on the first rose of summer
By an unseen hand wiped away.

Life rushes on like the rippling brook
That flows into the river.
It does not end, only passes at last
Into the sweet forever.

Life is indeed a great mystery
To those who travel its way,
Who never can reach its tomorrow
Or turn back to its yesterday.

For there's no way back to yesterday,
To the part of life that's gone.
Indeed a mystery, life passes once
O'er the road one travels on.

Life is a road with no ending
Twixt here and eternity's day.
It leads to the land of hereafter
Awaiting just over the way.

Life has its sorrow and heartaches,
But time is a healing balm
That soothes the heart with sweet music,
Touched by the words of a psalm.

Life has a great creator,
An artist of greatest renown.
He is seen in the rapturous beauty
In which the whole world is crowned.

He is seen in the fleecy billows
Adrift in the azure blue,
In the rainbow colors, the night bird's song,
He is known in the sunset hue.

Yes, life is a great mystery indeed,
But there's never a mystery
But what its own creator
Holds fast the golden key.

Rebirth

A spread of blue covering the sky,
Flung in space by God on high.
Tiny diamonds hold it tight,
Sparkling, glittering in the night.
Tiny snowflakes floating down
Softly kiss the dead dark ground,
Whispering soft a melody
Caressing gently, tenderly.
Golden sunshine high above
Smiling on the earth in love.
Sending sunbeams dancing bright
To chase away the frozen white.
Falling softly, silver rain,
Singing low a sweet refrain.
Crystal drops that woo the earth
To life again . . .a glad rebirth.

The Magic of Morning

There's magic in early morning
When the world is still asleep,
The dew is fresh on the roses,
And a mist hovers over the deep.
I watch the dark grow lighter
As the night shades fade away,
And a golden sunrise merges
With the dawn of a brand new day.
I sit alone in the stillness
And feel the peace it bring,
Like a silent benediction
Borne on angel wings.

Dreams

I'd like to follow the trails in the sky, made by the clouds as they slowly drift by.
I'd like to roam, when day is done, to the land in the midst of the setting sun.
I love the soft colors, the orange and the blue.
The painter is surely an artist true.
No colors on earth are there to behold that blend so well as the blue and the gold.
I'd like to walk down the Milky Way with those I see traveling at close of day-
An old man alone with staff in hand, as if he is seeking some far distant land.
I'd like to climb to the mountain height just as the moon comes out at night.
Ah breathless its beauty against the darkened sky,
Lighting the path for those who pass by.
I gaze spellbound, forgetting my care, at the tiny stars that twinkle there.
I wonder if the travelers who pass them by think they look like diamonds in the dark blue sky.
I'd like to live in that land I can see as I sit alone neath the willow tree.
O world of clouds drifting to and fro, who is the artist that made you so?

Alone In The Night

The night winds blow with air so soft.
The moon shines down in the warm hayloft,
And leaves me alone in the night.

Stars come out in the dark blue sky,
Dimmed by the shadows of clouds passing by,
And leaves me alone in the night.

The clouds make a picture above the blue yonder
Of pathways where weary travelers wander,
And leaves me alone in the night.

The song of the cricket is loud and drear
As it trips o'er the meadows and reaches my ear,
And leaves me alone in the night.

I see from afar the green willow trees.
Their long branches sway in the clear cool breeze,
And leaves me alone in the night.

My Heart's Window

When days are filled with sorrow,
Dark clouds hang overhead,
And crowding in upon me
A sense of pain and dread,
I see through my heart's window
The world God's hands have made;
The mountains and the valleys,
The trees that give forth shade.
I see the sun's still shining.
The flowers are still in bloom.
The birds are still singing.
Their melody fills the gloom.
So when my heart is aching,
I lift my eyes above,
And in the world around me
I see the beauty of God's love.
I fling my window open
And feel all nature's glow.
Its healing peace and beauty
Bring comfort to my soul.

He Pilots Me

He stilled the storms to a whisper.
The waves of the sea were hushed.

Matthew 4:39

Jesus, My Captain

Upon a great big ocean,
I sailed my ship one day.
But I had not chart or compass,
And soon I lost my way.
The nighttime gathered round me.
The shadows dark drew near.
The winds were high and threatening.
My heart soon filled with fear.

Alone on life's great ocean
With no captain near to guide,
No darkness then, nor tempest
Could my tears of anguish hide.
The storm swept in upon me.
It seemed my vessel tempest tossed
By the dashing waves about me
Would be forever lost.

For with none but me to steer her
Through the darkness to the shore,
I knew we could not make it
The troubled waters o'er.
But as we sailed in darkness
Upon the troubled sea,
I saw a lifeboat coming
With a Captain to rescue me.

And my little boat I could not steer,
With my captain's hand to guide,
Sailed peacefully to shore that day
O'er the ocean's angry tide.
The tempest tossed vessel was my life,
The ocean, the sea of sin.
The storms and winds were just a type
Of the storms that raged within

The lifeboat was salvation,
Jesus the captain and guide
Who steered my sin tossed vessel
Safely to the other side.
And still He is my captain
Life's troubled waters o'er,
And every day he's guiding me
Safe to the other shore.

The Fierce Old Storm

It stormed today on earth below.
The winds blew cold and fast.
The thunder roared. The sky grew dark.
The clouds their shadows cast.
The storm beat hard upon God's child,
Till he sought a place of rest
From the thunder's fearful roar,
From the winds and waves that pressed.

It stormed today on earth below.
God's child bowed low in prayer
To seek a refuge from the storm
That beat so fiercely there.
He cried aloud ere the winds blew cold,
Bowed low in a secret place,
And his cry reached right to the throne of God
As he sought the Savior's face.

It stormed today. Heaven's portals shook,
And as the wind raged fierce and wild,
The Savior stood near in infinite love
Lest the storm should harm his child.
While clouds were dark and winds swept high
On earth below today,
The Savior stood close by His child
And wiped the tears away.

It stormed today on earth below.
The Savior walked life's path again
Close by the side of His ransomed child,
And sheltered him there from the rain.
The storm was over on earth today.
No more its dark shadows cast.
God's child looked up from the secret place,
As the Savior whispered, "The storm is past."

The fiercest storm could not harm God's child.
It only made brighter the path he trod.
God's grace was sufficient, the fierce old storm
Only anchored more firmly his faith in God.
Oh fiercest storm and darkest clouds,
Oh winds that blow so wild,
Rage in all your fury on.
You cannot harm God's ransomed child

The Captain of My Soul

Over dark and dashing billows
My soul is tossed tonight.
The wind in raging fury blows;
The shore is not in sight.
But my soul has a Captain,
Though His face I cannot see.
Somewhere out in the darkness
His hand is guiding me.

It is He who sends a beacon
From yonder's distant shore,
To keep me safe within His care
The angry waters o'er.
And His eye is ever watchful
Lest my soul sink in despair
Neath the rolling, tossing billows,
Midst the ocean's angry snare.

The dark and dashing tempests toss;
The wind and billows blow;
The waves of life's dark waters sweep;
The thunders crack and roll.
But my Captain's name is Jesus,
And I see across the bay
He's sending out a beacon
To light the darkened way.

My soul no longer tosses.
The shore is now in view,
And o'er the stormy billows,
His face is shining through.
It is He who stills the tempest,
Makes the thunder cease to roll.
It is He who is forever
The Captain of my soul.

Pilot Me

I dreamed I was sailing on life's perilous sea,
Sailing so quickly to eternity.
The night was so dark that o'er shadowed me there,
And I was sinking in deep despair.
The wind blew cold, the waves swept high.
I wanted a friend, but none was nigh.
There was none to lead me, no hand to guide,
And no one to travel by my side.
I must go alone; my hopes were all lost.
Then I thought of Jesus and how He died on the cross.
And I looked up to heaven as I sailed life's sea,
And whispered, "Dear Jesus pilot me."
I looked, and lo I saw one stand
And o'er the waters stretch his hand.
I heard him whisper, "It is my will.
I'll pilot you child. Peace be still."

He was clothed in raiment of shining white,
And his face like an angel's was pure and bright.
He touched my hand as he stood on the sea,
And whispered, "I came to pilot thee."
"But I need a friend," I cried in despair,
"Someone who'll all my sorrows share."
He smiled and whispered, "Child I understand."
And oh so tenderly he took my hand.
He said, "I'll all your sorrows share.
Just cast on me your every care."
But I cried again. "Lord I need a guide."
He said, "Child forever I'll walk by your side."
I listened as He whispered, "It is my will."
And bade life's troubled waters Peace be still.
I watched him as he stood on life's perilous sea,
And I knew that he came to pilot me.

Seasons

To every thing there is a season, and a time to every purpose under the heaven:

Ecclesiastes 3:1

Christmas In My Heart

It is Christmas in my heart
When snow is on the ground,
And the world of frozen wonder
Is in glorious beauty found;
When sunshine breaks in splendor
On a world of dazzling white,
And snowflakes seem like diamonds
In the darkness of the night.

It is Christmas in my heart
When sunlight from above,
Upon each tiny blossom
Plants a tender kiss of love;
When the earth awakes from slumber,
And birds begin to sing;
When trees with leaves are budding,
And the world is dressed in spring.

It is Christmas in my heart
When days are hot and long,
And nighttime brings the music
Of the cricket's mournful song;
When flowers bloom in splendor
With colors rare and bright,
And shadows of the evening
Bring the cool, sweet air of night.

It is Christmas in my heart
When the world is dressed in brown,
And leaves in merry laughter
Come dancing to the ground;
When God paints the earth with colors
Of breathless beauty rare,
And the pungent smell of autumn,
With fragrance fills the air.

It is Christmas in my heart
Through each season of the year,
Since Jesus came and filled my life
One day with Christmas cheer.
The light that shined so long ago
On a stable bed of hay,
Bringing hope to a world in darkness
That long past Christmas day,

Has shined down through the ages
To a world in dark despair,
Giving hope and joy and gladness
To all men everywhere.
And the Christ born in a manger
To save man from his sin,
Now lives each day within my heart
And gives me peace within.

Christ On Trial

I dreamed Christ was put on trial,
And I to the witness stand
Was called to speak for the Master
A word at the Judge's command.
There all the disciples and prophets,
Peter, John and Paul,
And all those who knew the Master
Were to speak at the Judge's call.

Could anyone find fault with Him
As he stood on trial that day?
Jesus Christ, the Son of God.
I heard the Judge then say,
"Simon Peter please come forth.
Tell me, what do you know of this man?"
I saw Peter then walk up
And touch the Master's hand.

I saw his tear-filled eyes grow dim,
As I heard him softly say,
"I met this man called Jesus
On Galilee's shores one day.
I followed close beside Him,
And He sweetly talked with me.
I watched Him heal the sick, raise the dead,
And make the blind to see.

Then one day I denied Him,
As along life's path I trod,
But He so sweetly forgave me.
Truly He is the Son of God."
Then I saw John the Revelator
Take his place at the witness stand.
I heard his quickly saying,
"I've naught against this man.

For he bade me follow Him one day,
Though long I'd wandered far.
He's Jesus Christ the Son of God,
The bright and morning star."
Then the Judge's voice I heard again,
"Thomas, please take your place."
I saw Thomas then walk up
And look on the Master's face.

I heard him tell how he doubted
Till Jesus appeared that day,
Bade him feel his side and feet and hands.
Then the Judge went on to say,
"Judas. Judas please come forth
Take your place at the witness stand."
Then sobbing and weeping Judas spoke.
"I've betrayed an innocent man."

Silence. Then Paul went forth.
He told how on the Damascus way
God had shown a shining light
Across his path that day.
Then I saw the master smile
As more of the story Paul gave, for he declared,
"There's no other name under heaven
Whereby we must be saved."

Then the Judge called Pilate
To come to the witness stand.
Pilot spoke, "Mocked, scorned and hated
In the Judgment hall stood this man,
But he answered not a word
Midst the rioting and dim.
Though others seemed to all find fault,
I could find no fault in him."

Then I listened so intently.
The Judge has called my name.
What could I say of this man called Jesus?
My face grew red with shame.
With faltering voice I cried aloud,
"I once was lost in sin.
Then this man Jesus passed my way
And gave me peace within."

Suddenly I knew just what to do.
I walked to the witness stand
And over to where Jesus stood,
And tenderly I took His hands.
I lifted them up so the Judge could see
As I pointed to the nail prints there.
Through tears I cried, "It was all for me,
The cross that he did bear."

I showed hem how His shoulders
Were bent with toil and care.
I touched his weary sacred brow
As I pointed to the thorn prints there.
I told them how his side was pierced.
I cried, "It was for me
He bled and died upon the cross
In pain and agony."

Then I saw the Master smile
As tears of joy did flow.
"To me, He's the lily of the valley," I cried.
"Fairest of ten thousands to my soul.
He's the fountain of living waters,
The bread of life to me,
The beginning and the ending
Through all eternity."

"He's the bright and morning star," I cried,
"The rose of Sharon fair,
The light of my salvation
As I walk the way down here.
My rock, my guide, my pilot
When billows o'er me roll,
My help, my hope, my comforter.
He's the lover of my soul."

And if Christ were put on trial,
And you to the witness stand
Were called to speak for the Master
A word at the Judge's command.
Would you find fault in all He's done
For you along life's way?
If Christ should be put on trial,
What would you say today?

Where Jesus Died

The old rugged cross! I can see it now
As it stands there alone on Golgotha's brow.
How blessed! How sacred its blood stained side!
The old rugged cross where Jesus died.
A light from Heaven sheds abroad its glow
On that old rugged cross that all my know
That a Savior died on that cross one day,
For all the world the ransom did pay.
See there's a spear, on the ground it lies,
Forgotten now beneath the darkened skies.
There's the prints where they nailed His hands,
And if you look more closely to where the rugged cross stands,
You'll see there's drops of blood where He lay,
Dying for you and me that day.
I see the footprints where people gathered around
Some weeping, some mocking as they knelt on the ground,
Their eyes fixed on Jesus as He hung on the cross,
Dying in their stead, paying the cost.
Oh blessed Savior keep me near
The old rugged cross as I journey here.
Keep me ever near; help me to feel
Thy sanctifying power as before it I kneel.
For on its form you died for me,
That I from sin might be set free.
May I always see how you paid the cost
When you died in my stead on the old rugged cross.

The Empty Tomb

It was quiet on that morning,
The mob had ceased to cry
With voices rough and boisterous,
"Crucify Him! Let him die."
Now they spoke in signs and gestures,
Their voices hushed and low.
Now and then the sound of weeping
From those who loved him so.

They had followed him so closely
Up Calvary's hill that day,
And watched him broken hearted
As he stumbled on the way.
Watched as those Roman soldiers
Nailed their savior to the cross,
And each pounding of the hammer
Brought an awful sense of loss.

The earth shook and trembled,
And darkness settled round.
They shook with fear and wonder
As His blood dripped to the ground.
It seemed hope was gone forever.
God the Father hid his face.
He couldn't bear to watch man's savior
Dying there in such disgrace.

They listened. He was speaking
As the blood flowed from His side,
"It is finished now forever."
Then He hung his head and died.
And man's part then was finished
Of God's great salvation plan.
It was started up in heaven,
Through Calvary brought to man.

The cross now stands a symbol,
And has for ages past,
Of suffering, pain and sorrow,
Of death's dark shadows cast.
Three days, and they came at morning,
Hearts filled with hope and fear.
An angel spoke these words of victory,
"Behold He is not here!

He has risen as He promised.
He has conquered death and sin.
And he lives to walk beside you,
Lives to give you peace within."
And their hearts were stirred within them
When he met them on the way,
And gave to them this promise,
"I'll come back again some day."

The empty tomb stands a symbol,
Not of death or sin or gloom,
But eternal life through Jesus.
Thank God for that empty tomb.
It brought hope and peace and comfort
With the dawning of that day.
For God's great plan was finished
When the stone was rolled away.

The Stone Was Rolled Away

If on that long past morning
They'd come in twilight gloom
And found the stone still blocking
The entrance to the tomb,
No angels there to greet them,
No words of comfort spoken,
But soldiers armed and guarding
The seal still unbroken.
Then the tomb would have no meaning,
No glory in the cross,
And man still steeped in darkness,
Would be forever lost.

But oh! The tomb was empty!
An angel standing there
Dispelled the death and darkness,
And light shone everywhere.
For Christ our Lord was risen
As He promised in His word.
The angel's voice rejoicing
Was the first sound they heard.
In humble adoration
Let our hearts rejoice today,
Because the tomb was empty.
The stone was rolled away.

He's Alive!

There was a garden, a perfect place
Filled with time and endless space.
A beautiful garden with flowers rare
And song birds singing everywhere.

No darkness there the mind could trace,
No death or dying in that place.
But all was filled with peace and love,
And heaven's light shown from above.

But in that garden one day there crept
A fearsome foe while nature slept.
With flattering words he then beguiled,
Deceived, destroyed God's innocent child.

There was a garden long years ago.
Filled with agony and woe,
Where God's own son prayed and wept,
While those he loved beyond him slept.

There in agony and pain
He prayed till the sun came up again.
Then he arose from tear drenched sod,
Surrendered completely himself to God.

There was a hillside where could be seen
Three crosses towering above the green,
And trudging up the dusty sod,
The sacrificial Lamb of God.

Between two thieves they hung their King.
And lo! The birds refused to sing.
As darkness all around descended,
The voice of God cried, "It is ended."

There was a garden in the gloom,
And in it was a brand new tomb.
There they buried Him that day.
Left him there and went away.

There dawned a morning clear and bright
And earth was filled with heaven's light.
All nature woke from sleep that day,
And death and darkness fled away.

While the earth shook and trembled,
The mighty host of heaven assembled.
Their song rang out through time and space,
As the Son of God took His rightful place.

The message rang through all the ages,
To rich and poor, to kings and sages.
Salvation's price is paid for now,
For all who at His feet will bow,

Will find new life and hope within,
Forgiveness from their every sin.
For the tomb could not hold Him prey.
He conquered death and hell that day.

And echoing through the ages long,
All nature sings the victor's song.
The cry is heard from shore to shore,
"He's alive! He's alive forevermore!

Old Glory

Old Glory stands straight and tall
For all the world to see,
A symbol of the USA,
The land of liberty.
The red exemplifies the blood
Of those who fought and fell
In foreign land, on bloody soil
In the midst of war and hell.

The white exemplifies the tears
Cried in the dark of night,
Wrung from those who stayed and prayed
For those who went to fight.
The blue stands for loyalty
Of hearts true and brave,
And those who lie forever dead
In a lonely bloody grave.

Beside Old Glory stands a cross
For all the world to see,
A symbol of the love of Christ
Who died to set man free.
And naught can wash away the stain
Of blood shed on that day,
Nor hide the power of that hour
That showed to man the way.

The cross now stands for freedom,
The red, the white, the blue,
For each man to worship
What he believes is true.
May we guard it bravely
That all may ever see
The blessed Christ of Calvary
Who died to set man free.

Memories

Every good gift and every perfect gift is from above,
and comes down from the Father of light,
with whom there is no variation or shadow of turning.

James 1:17 (NIV)

Sometimes I Remember

Sometimes I remember
On a lazy summer day,
An old porch swing a creaking,
Two little girls at play.
All dressed up in finery,
High heels and sheer silk hose,
Gathered so discreetly
From mom's discarded clothes.
We wrapped our dolls in blankets,
Pretended they were real,
Gave them hugs and kisses
We knew they could not feel.

Sometimes I remember
A huge old maple tree
Where we sat beneath its branches,
Making memories, you and me.
In a yard with bare brown patches
Scattered here and there
And yellow dandelions
Growing everywhere.
We ate from tiny dishes,
And swept a sweepless floor.
We drank our cup of make believe
Back in those days of yore.

Sometimes I remember
Through it's been so many years,
When we shared our deepest secrets,
Our laughter and our tears.
And like the golden thread of love
That bound us way back then,
So memories seem to draw me back
To that land of let's pretend.
I'd like to be a child again,
If only for a day
And spend those cherished times with you,
When we were girls at play.

Precious Memories

We all have precious memories
That we treasure day by day
Of cherished spots and places
As we walk along life's way;

Of words once softly whispered
That live within our heart,
Of loved ones true and precious
With whom we've had to part.

And to my heart this moment
There comes a thought of you
Like the tender touch of sunshine
On a meadow fresh with dew.

And among life's many memories
That I hold so dear today
Are the times we spent together
Before you went away.

My Brother Jim

He always had a cheery smile, my brother Jim,
Though life, with all its many cares was seldom kind to him.
He never told a hard luck tale as many others would.
But always had a friendly word, and did the best he could.

He couldn't walk like you and me; he had to limp along.
But he faced life as it came to him and always had a song.
Through the cold days of winter, his body racked with pain,
He longed for warmth and sunshine of spring to come again.

My heart just will not question, though I often wonder why
The dark clouds seemed to linger and hide the sunlit sky.
For God, in His great wisdom, who always knows the best,
Took Jim home one day to a land of peace and rest.

In that land of springtime, where the sunlight ne'er grows dim,
And the song birds sing forever, I'll meet my brother Jim.
We'll walk those golden streets with a step that's sure and true,
To part no more forever in that land beyond the blue.

A Child. A Man

A little scrap of paper!
I almost threw it away.
A broken toy . . . a battered thing
As I cleaned my house one day.
They seemed to be in the way.

But to my mind came an image
Of a small boy hard at play,
Touching with care the battered toy,
As he played throughout the day.
"Please don't throw them away."

So I laid them tenderly on the shelf
To keep them for a while.
He slipped his little hand in mine,
And gave me a loving smile.
"I'm glad you understand."

Now another day, another year
I found the battered toy
Together with a heap of things
That belonged to a little boy.
I held them in my hand.

Should I throw them away?
I hugged them to my heart.
They held such precious memories
That I felt the teardrops start.
"I'll discard them if I can."

Then a manly voice I heard
Speak from the open door.
"Throw them away." He smiled at me.
"I don't need them any more.
I've grown to be a man."

The Roses Are Blooming

The roses are blooming again
Outside the kitchen door,
Creeping over the garden rail
Onto the cement floor.

They're growing in quiet profusion,
Blooming in simple grace,
Bending the laden branches,
Adorning the old home place.

Their fragrance fills the summer air
That creeps in the open door.
But someone else enjoys them now,
For they are mine no more.

It seems strange that I have moved
From the old house on the hill
To another place that's best for me
Where all is quiet and still,

Where I can watch the world go by,
Content to let it be,
While I enjoy sweet fellowship
Between my Lord and me.

Someday I will move again
From this old house of clay
To a place where deep red roses grow
For one eternal day.

It seems not strange for me to hope
This one last home of mine
Will be blest with fragrant roses
About the door entwined.

Memories of You

Almost five years have passed since you were here,
Since I heard your voice and saw your face.
Your loving ways and gentle words
I know I can never replace.
Memories fond come back to me
Of times when you were here,
Of when I put my hand in yours,
Of evenings fond and dear.

I see you now sitting by the fire
In your favorite rocking chair,
With your foot propped up on the old coal stove,
Rocking with never a care.
And down through the ages,
When your hair was turning white,
And your eyes were gaining that far away look
That peers beyond the night;

When wrinkles appeared on your forehead,
And your hands were rough and old,
It all led up to that awful day
They buried your there in the cold.
And now that you're gone, I've thought
Of the times that used to be,
And longed for the days of long ago
When you were here with me.

Your Friendship

Robins accompany springtime.
Flowers come with May.
Evening brings the sunset,
And sunrise brings the day.

There are many, many blessings
Sent from the Father's hand
To comfort, help and guide us
Ere we reach the promised land.

So knowing you brings happiness,
Sweet and pure and true,
Like a blessing sent from heaven,
Or a meadow fresh with dew.

It's our Father's hand that guides us,
And one day our ways may part,
But the blessing of your friendship
Will linger in my heart.

Love

When I lay groping in the cold maze of depression,
You covered me with the blanket of your love,
Smoothing the wrinkled edges,
Coaxing the twisted pieces into shape.
When faith was just a flickering flame
You fanned it slowly, faithfully
Till it burst into a blaze. When I prayed for death,
Your song pierced the shell of my despair
And gave me life. When I learned the power
Of a mother's love, you snuggled close to God
And went to sleep.

Heaven and Home

And God shall wipe away all tears from their eyes; and there shall be no more death, neither sorrow, nor crying, neither shall there be any more pain: for the former things are passed away.
And he that sat upon the throne said, Behold, I make all things new. And he said unto me, Write: for these words are true and faithful.

Revelation 21:4 - 5 (NIV)

I'll Be Home

Please don't weep for me my friend,
When at last I'm laid to rest,
And my body lies to be viewed by all
In funeral garments dressed.
For that'll not be me your eyes behold,
But just an empty shell.
I will have long since been at home
With those I love so well.

I'll not need earthly garments there,
For a robe of spotless white,
I'll wear through all eternity
In a land where comes no night.
I'll be walking golden streets up there,
Where fields of glory wave.
O I tell you now it won't be me
You'll bury in a grave.

There may be many flowers here
To grace my funeral room,
To fill the air with fragrance sweet
And chase away the gloom.
But I'll have miles and miles up there
Of flowers sweet and rare,
Lilies fair and lilacs bright
Whose fragrance fills the air.

The flowers here so soon will die.
They'll wither and decay.
The fragrance once so fresh and sweet
Will forever fade away.
But flowers there bloom forever
They never fade and die,
For death can never enter in
Those gates of pearl on high.

Here I oft must say goodbye
To friends along the way.
But there we'll meet to part no more
In a land of endless day.
No winter winds will blow up there.
No hearts will long for spring.
For there the sun forever shines.
The birds forever sing.

No endless nights of dark despair.
All sorrow there will cease.
Within that summer land above.
All is joy and peace.
So if you must weep, then weep for joy,
For I'll be gone, my friend
To a better land, my home sweet home,
Where joys will never end.

A Sunrise Is Coming

When shadows of night gather round me
And the sun sinks to rest again,
I think of the journey before me;
I think of the prize I must win.
And my heart cries aloud in the stillness
To a Savior who knows every care,
"Keep me faithful a little while longer.
Help me to enter that city so fair."

Then to my heart comes a whisper.
It bids all my sorrows to flee.
It fills all the darkness around me.
"My grace is sufficient for thee."
There's many a rugged battle;
There's many a rough dark road.
But His presence shall always be with me.
His strong arm shall bear all my load.

The journey is almost over,
And the battle is nearly won.
There's a sunrise that is waiting o'er yonder
Just at the set of life's sun.
There's a daybreak that's surely coming,
Where nighttime comes never more.
And I mean to welcome its dawning
With Jesus on Heaven's fair shore

That Is Home

Have you ever stood at the close of day
And viewed the lights just o'er the way?
And you knew that somewhere over there
Were home and loved ones and friends that care

And a longing rose within your heart
That made the tears to almost start.
And somehow deep inside you knew
Those lights from home were calling you.

I'm just a traveler on life's way,
Traveling toward the close of day.
On yonder shore by faith I see
Those lights that seem to beckon me.

A Savior's voice by faith I hear.
He whispers softly, "Do not fear.
You see those lights just o'er the way?
There lies a land of endless day.

So keep your eyes upon that shore
Where pain and death will come no more.
For soon will come the close of day,
And that is home just o'er the way."

Where The Weary Are At Rest

Here the wicked often trouble
Till I almost think it vain
As I strive for heaven's portals
And the prize I long to gain.
But the sweetest voice then whispers
As I kneel alone and pray,
"Never mind the rugged journey.
I'll go with you all the way."

Here oftimes my heart is heavy,
And my head bows low with care,
Till it seems my every burden
Not an earthly friend will share.
But a still, small voice then whispers,
And once more my heart is blessed.
Tells me of that land eternal
Where the weary are at rest.

Oft the dark clouds gather 'round me
Till my soul looks up in fear
Lest the tossing waves about me
Bow me down in deep despair.
Then I hear the sweetest music,
I see the light once more,
And the sweetest peace and comfort
Seem to drift from heaven's shore.

O sweetest land of bliss eternal
For thy courts I often sigh,
Where the wicked never trouble
And no tears can dim the eye.
Where the trials cease forever
And the heavy heart is blessed.
Where the storm clouds never bother,
And the weary are at rest.

When at last this life is over,
And I strive no more to gain
That eternal prize forever
That one time seemed so in vain,
Then I'll be with Christ my Savior
In that land that's free from stress,
Where the wicked never trouble
And the weary are at rest.

Life's Eventide

When the sun sinks to rest at the close of time,
And the toils of life are o'er,
I think of a day in a land far away
That will last forever more.
Midst the toils and suffering, and cares of life,
Midst the bondage of Satan's snare;
Sweet peace o'er my soul like the sea billows roll,
When I think of that city so fair.
Though discouragement may come, my pathway grow dim,
No light from the lighthouse I see;
One moment in Heaven and one glimpse of Him
Worth all of my trials will be.
Though tears fill my eyes and my head hangs low,
And loneliness surrounds me here;
Someday by His grace I shall look on His face.
His hand will brush away every tear.
And once I'm inside that city of gold,
And the saints of all ages I see
I'll join in the song with the blood-washed throng
And sing through eternity.

If There Were Tears In Heaven

If there were tears in heaven
And we could cry up there,
Cry for joy and gladness
Within that city fair;
I'd like to talk it o'er with Jesus,
And while He tells me the reason why,
I'd like to sit there at His feet
And cry, and cry, and cry.

Now some folks laugh when they're happy,
And some with words explain,
But I find when I'm the happiest
The tears I can't contain.
When I shout o'er the hills of glory
With my Savior walking nigh,
If there were tears in heaven
I'd cry, and cry, and cry.

When I stand with the blood-washed throng
I know the tears would start.
When I tell redemption's story
And about the peace within my heart;
When I behold Him face to face
He who saved my soul from sin,
If there were tears in heaven,
I know I'd cry again.

If there were tears in heaven,
Within those portals sweet,
I know they'd fall as I worship
There at my Savior's feet.
But since we can't cry in heaven,
And the tears can never start
There must be words enough up there
To express what's in my heart.

A Kingdom Unknown

A part of me lies in a kingdom unknown,
A kingdom just over the sea
Where the lights that are bright in the dark of the night
Seem to be calling to me.

My heart within me beats wild with desire,
And my eyes grow misty with tears.
I long to enter that kingdom that lies
Beyond the passing of years.

I reach feeble hands toward that kingdom unknown,
That kingdom just over the sea.
I whisper the names of those gone before
Who are nearest and dearest to me.

And somehow I know when the long night is past,
And the shadows give place to the day,
My soul shall live on in that kingdom unknown
That lies at the end of the way.

There Is A Haven

Somewhere in the vast unknown future,
Untouched by the fingers of pain,
Unkissed by the harsh lips of sorrow,
Is a place my soul longs for in vain.
Is it wrong to long for a haven
Where disappointment ne'er shows its sad face,
Where pain cannot greet its victim,
And sorrow ne'er leave its sad trace?

Hush my soul! Be quiet within me!
A faint whisper I fancy I hear,
Nor cry out so loud for that haven
Where cometh no sorrow or fear.
A voice? Yes! I hear its sweet echo
In the song that the sparrows sing.
Tells me somewhere there is a haven.
My soul does not long for in vain.

There is no pain in that haven.
The leaves falling round me here
Tell me it's true, and I know it.
There's no pain in that haven fair.
The cold harsh lips of sorrow
Can ne'er kiss its tender brow,
And my soul reaches out in anguish
To touch it, to reach, just now.

A haven somewhere in the future.
A goal to be reached, then I'll rest.
I feel it in the rapturous beauty
In which the world around me is dressed.
I hear it, and my heart hums a melody
In a language no mortal can speak;
A haven that lies deep within me.
My soul no longer shall seek

A Little Farther On

I lost my friend today.
While angels hovered near
To comfort loved ones dear,
God bore her safe away.

He held her close in death,
And in that mystic night
Gave her eternal light
And His eternal breath.

She is not really gone.
I see through shadows dim
She's walking close to Him
A little farther on.

Face To Face

When twilight descends in curtains of gray
And covers with dust the light of day;
When clover fields sleep beneath the hovering mist,
The rivers and mountains with darkness are kissed;
Then in my heart a longing is born
For a far away heaven, a golden morn.
My heart is quickened, and my soul is awake
With thoughts of a journey I know I must take.

When shades of white creep into view,
And blend golden sunlight with the shimmering dew;
When dawn spreads its greetings` in splashes of red,
And the glory of morning breaks over my head;
My soul shall burst forth from this vessel of clay,
And soar to that heaven just over the way.
Then bathed in the beauty of love and of grace,
I'll see my dear savior face to face.

Jesus, My Savior

My heart is rejoicing. There's coming a day
When life with its sorrows will all pass away.
Then eternity's morning with burst into view,
At last a reality for me and for you.
When free from its shackles, my soul then shall soar
To that city eternal on yonder fair shore.
I don't care about the mansion, or the sights to behold.
I don't care about the pearly gates or the streets of pure gold.
I'll run past the tree of life, past the pure flowing springs.
I'll run past the angels with gossamer wings.
I'll run past the prophets I'm longing to see,
Past all my loved ones who are waiting for me.
I'll run straight to Jesus down a pure golden street.
In unspeakable wonder, I'll fall at his feet,
And shout loud his praises in a world without end.
My Jesus, my Savior, my lover, my friend.

Just Beyond

Just beyond this night of darkness lies a land of endless day.
With eyes of faith I see it past the turning of the way.
There loved ones wait to great me. Our hands shall clasp again.
In the midst of joy and blessing, we'll forget the night of pain.

Just beyond this vale of sorrow is a land that's free from care.
With tear filled eyes I see it beyond the sunset, over there.
And I'm walking ever towards it as I journey day by day.
Its golden rays of sunshine guide my footsteps on the way.

Just beyond this lonely journey, my home is waiting me.
Sometime it seems so distant faith's eye can barely see.
But the hope that lies within me sees the lights along the shore,
And somehow I seem to know that my journey's almost o'er.

Death Is

Death is only a gateway out of a stormy night
Into a day of peace and calm, into a land of light.

Death is a door that opens into a garden fair,
Filled with lovely flowers and precious jewels rare;

A garden full of roses where little children play,
And no darkness ever enters to mar the light of day.

Death is a golden stairway in the corridors of time,
Where angels guard the entrance to a land of bright sunshine.

Death is a beautiful sunset that lights up the western skies
And slips away to shine anew, in a land of eternal sunrise.

Death is a ship that passes to sail life's sea no more,
But pulls into the harbor on Heaven's golden shore.

Death

I stood alone one evening beside a rippling brook.
The sun was setting over the western horizon.
The dark clouds, mingled with the rapturous hue
Of the setting sun, cast a spell o'er the world about me.
The breathless beauty of the blue and gold
Portrayed the skill of a great artist.
As I followed the trail made by the touch
Of his great brush, my heart longed to meet
This artist face to face. I watched,
Silent with wonder, as the blue and gold
Of the western sky bore the weary old sun
Tenderly to its resting place.

I stood alone one morning in the early twilight.
The bright sun was peeping
Over the eastern horizon.
The same blue and gold that laid it to rest,
Now with outstretched arms,
Welcomed it appearing, and I thought,
"When I as a weary traveler
Have finished my labor on this earth,
I too, shall be borne to my resting place
And welcomed on another shore
Even by the great artist who had painted
So beautiful a picture.

Prayer And Solitude

But you, when you pray, go into your room, and when you have shut your door, pray to your Father who is in the secret place; and your Father who sees in secret will reward you openly.

Matthew 6:6 (NIV)

Secret Place of Prayer

O precious secret place of prayer,
I would, within your portals sweet
Soar up beyond life's toil and care,
Sitting low at Jesus' feet.
O could I just enfolded be
Within your courts alone,
Reaching up, God's face to see,
And touch, at last, His throne.

O precious secret place of prayer,
Still for your courts I sigh.
Bear me up on wings of love.
To God's bosom draw me nigh.
You are a channel to His throne,
A path that leads above,
And safe within your courts I rest,
Enfolded in his love.

I Leave It There With Him

I know a shortcut to the throne of God;
A key to answered pray.
I just talk with Him each day
And leave my burden there.
His marvelous grace is always mine
When the path I walk grows dim.
In dark of night or morning bliss,
The secret to it all is this:
I leave it there with him.

Alone With God

When cares of life are thronging,
In my hears there comes a longing;
A longing just to be alone with God.

When shades of night are falling,
And temptations strong are calling,
I want to walk the path my Savior trod.

When on life's pathway dreary,
My heart grows sad and weary,
I want so much to be on heaven's shore.

O Savior keep my heart from sin,
Help me dear Lord the victory win,
And let me live with you forevermore.

My Prayer

When daylight fades and shades of gray
Invade my soul,
May your love overshadow me.
When dark earth's light of silver prisms
Penetrate the night,
May I rest in your love.
When golden rays of dawn vibrate
The twilight of my soul,
May I awaken in your presence.

Blessed Quietness

A blessed holy quietness
Fills my troubled soul,
Calms the pain and aching there
That one time had control.
A precious sweet serenity
Inspired by God above
Shields me from all evil
And hides me in His love.

Now the pain and sorrow
That one time filled my breast
Are borne away on angel wings
And lost in His sweet rest.
The wounds that once were made
By hatred, doubt and fear,
He touched with Gilead's healing balm
And made them disappear.

The clouds that marred my path,
And made the way seem rough
Scattered fast when He stepped in
And said, "It is enough."
Oh quiet peace eternal
That stills the raging storms,
I want to rest forevermore
Safe in my Father's arms.

I Said A Prayer For You

I said a prayer for you today
While the morning light was dim.
I asked that God would keep you safe
And draw you close to Him.
I asked that He would take your hand
And guide you o'er life's way.
While all the world was sound asleep,
I prayed for you today.

I asked that God would lift the load
That lay upon your heart,
Fill your soul with peace and joy
And bid your cares depart.
So if your load has lighter grown,
And your skies are not as gray,
Just know it's all because He cares
And answers prayer today.

Because of the Rain

I stood in the heat of the day
Looking at my garden.
The sun, shining down
On an already parched ground,
Together with the lack of rain
Caused the earth to crack
And the flowers to droop.
A clap of thunder! A flash of lightning!
I ran for shelter
As the rain came pouring down.

I stood in the heat of the day
Looking at my garden.
The ground was rich and fertile.
The flowers stood straight and tall,
Faces lifted, toward the sky,
Raindrops glistened on the flowers.
Oh Lord! My soul is so dry.
My head is hanging low.
Please send the refreshing rain.
Let it fall upon my soul.

You Know What's Best For Me

I am talking to You, Jesus
Though I find no words to speak,
My heart is softly praying
As the tears roll down my cheek.
I don't know what to ask Lord,
It seems to be in vain
To hope for peace and freedom
From this awful sense of pain.
As I bow alone before you,
Somehow inside I know
That someday, in your own time,
Your peace will calm my soul.
I know you have a reason,
Though I don't understand.
I lift my heart in worship
And give to you my hand.
I trust that you will guide me
Over paths I cannot see,
Content that in your wisdom
You know what's best for me.

Gethsemane

I have been to Gethsemane's garden
When day was as black as night,
And Satan in hostile fury
Tried to distort my sight.
I've knelt alone in obscurity,
Prayed through the midnight hour,
Till my tears made a puddle about me.
And my soul felt void of power.

I've wrestled alone in the darkness
Till there was no more of me,
And God's face within the shadows
Was the only face I could see.
I've emptied my soul of its burden
In surrender, bitter sweet.
I've felt His touch of approval
And knew that my life was complete.

I'm Growing Old

Lord, I'm not a little girl anymore
Full of pep and energy.
My steps have grown shaky and slow.
My hands feel weak and trembling;
I can't seem to steady them anymore.
This body is growing old.
But I'm not old inside, Lord.
I feel as small and helpless
As I did years ago.
I still want to snuggle close to you
And feel loved and sheltered.
I still feel that zeal to work for you,
To climb mountains, to win battles.
So Lord, forget that this body
Is growing old,
And find a place for me
In your vineyard.

Pray To Your Father In Secret

Pray to your Father in secret.
Make your ways known unto Him,
And your Father which sees in secret
Will help you the battle to win.
Tell Him your soul's deep desires.
Let the tears unheeded start,
And your Father which sees in secret
Will grant the desires of your heart.
Tell Him your troubles and problems.
Tell Him the ills that beset,
And your Father which hears in secret
Will never forsake or forget.
Oh pray to your Father in secret.
Ne'er from His presence depart,
And your Father who loves you dearly
Will keep you close to His heart.

Solitude

God gave the gift of loneliness.
I held it close to me.
I laid my head upon its breast;
There I found sweet peace and rest
That others could not see.
In that quiet solitude
My heart was touched with grace,
And in its glow
That filled my soul,
I saw the Master's face.

Trust In Me And Rest

When the silence of dawn
Creeps through the day
And blends with the stillness of night,
I hear a sweet voice
Speak through the quiet,
"I am here child,
My arms are around you;
My Spirit is within you;
And my love overshadows you.
Trust in Me and rest.

Rest

When loneliness pain and heartache
Are more than you can bear,
And there seems to be no answer
When you call on Him in prayer;
When clouds obscure the brightness,
And darkness hides His face;
When yesterday's song is ended,
And sorrows fills its place;
Just snuggle close to Jesus,
Lay your heard upon His breast,
Feel His arms around you,
Close your eyes and rest.

A Friend In Jesus

I love to be quiet before Him,
Waiting at his feet.
To feel His presence near
Makes my live complete.
What joy to know He's leading
Though dark the way may be,
And that His hand is guiding
Over paths I cannot see.
I love to kneel before him
And hear his still small voice,
For in the darkest hours
It makes my heart rejoice.
A sinner once I wandered.
No hope, no peace within.
Then I fell in love with Jesus,
And He saved my soul form sin.
He's a friend above all others.
Oh what fellowship divine
Just to know He is abiding.
I am His and He is mine.

There Is A Place By Me

When storms of life are raging
And winter winds are cold;
When there is no light about me,
No earthly hand to hold;
When loved ones have forgotten;
Their face I cannot see,
I hear my Savior whisper,
"There is a place by me.
I made it especially for you
A long, long time ago
Before you felt the chill
Of winter winds that blow.
So snuggle close beside me.
And dry the tears that start.
For all is peace and comfort
In your place within my heart."

On Jesus' Breast

Did you ever hear, when storms raged near,
A sweet voice whisper in your ear?
"When through the test, you've tried your best,
Child lay your head upon My breast.

When on sinking sand you may seem to stand,
No man can pluck you from My hand."
Oh could we learn to Him to turn
When our hearts for love and peace doth yearn.

And on His breast find peace and rest
Sheltered safe from trials and tests.
And could we know the winds that blow
Can never harm our ransomed soul.

For sheltered there from every care
Our burdens are not hard to bear.
There's sweet release and sorrows cease.
On Jesus' breast all is at peace.

Garden Of My Heart

I've a garden that lies secluded
Far from the world apart
Where I walk when day is ended.
It's the garden of my heart.
There I meet with Christ my Savior
In the early morning light,
When the gentle rays of sunshine
Bid farewell to darkest night.

There I tell Him all my troubles
And give Him all my care.
There I feel His benediction
As I bow alone in prayer.
Though the storm about me rages
And the winds in fury blow,
All is peaceful in my garden
Where the sweetest flowers grow.

They are planted by the Master,
Watered by His love,
Kissed with golden sunlight
That shines from Heaven above.
From a busy world secluded,
I love to walk each day
Where the flowers bloom forever
On a golden sunlit way.

Where the darkness never enters
To hide His blessed face,
And the storms that sometimes gather
Are filled with wondrous grace.
Sheltered from life's busy highways
While the world goes rushing by,
I'm glad I have a garden
Where we walk, just He and I

Safe On Jesus' Breast

A few short years ago
When just a child at play,
My heart would oft grow weary
With the childish cares of day.
Then my feet would homeward turn,
And I'd find a place of rest
From all my childish woes and hurts,
Safe on Mother's breast.

Then my heart would sob the problem
To a mother's listening ear,
Till with a hand of kindness
She would brush away each tear.
And somehow my problems vanished,
And it seemed to be all right.
For just to snuggle close to mother
Calmed the darkest hours of night.

A few short years have passed since then.
Now I walk the narrow way,
And oft-times my heart grows weary
With the toils and cares of day,
Till with tears of inward anguish
I seek a place of rest
From the raging storms about me.
Safe on Jesus' breast.

My heart then sobs the problem
To a Father's listening ear,
Till with a hand of tender kindness
He brushes away each tear,
And somehow my problems vanish,
And it seems to be all right.
For just to snuggle close to Jesus
Calms the darkest hours of night.

Friend if you're discouraged,
Bowed beneath a weight of care,
Seek a place alone with Jesus;
You will find a solace there.
Storms can never harm you.
Cares cannot molest,
For all is safe alone with Jesus
With your head upon His breast.

When I Snuggle Close To Him

When the twilight shadows deepens
And the night time closes in,
I feel a tug upon my heart strings
Steal across the shadows dim.
I want to spend some time with Jesus,
Lift my heart to Him in prayer.
I want to feel His love enfold me
In His tender loving care.
All my friends and loved ones
Fade into the shadows dim
When I am alone with Jesus
And I snuggle close to Him.

There Is A Place In Jesus

There is a place in Jesus
Where the raging storms of life
Cannot cause my faith to waver
Or bring one moment's strife.
Where the storms that beat around me
And the raging winds that blow
Cannot mar my faith in Jesus
Nor harm my ransomed soul.

There's a shelter from the dangers
That come to me each day
To lure me from the path of duty
And turn me from the narrow way.
There is a place in Jesus
That's meant for only me
Where sorrows cannot touch me
And the dark clouds have to flee.

A place of peace and quiet
Where I alone can stand
And look out across the mountain
To that golden summer-land.
A place where heaven beckons
And loved ones wait for me,
Just beyond that last great sunset,
Just beyond the crystal sea.

By faith I mean to make it
When this earthly race is run,
When the trials of life are finished,
And the battles fought and won.
I mean to stand before Him
On that last great judgment day,
And know I have been faithful
Till the ending of life's way.

Encouragement

I am with you always,
even to the end of the world.

Matthew 28:20b

I will never leave you
nor forsake you.

Hebrews 13:5b

Safe In The Rock of Ages

I asked him to forgive my sins,
To calm the raging wild.
He tenderly drew me to His heart
And made me then His child.
I asked that He'd supply my need
Through every passing day.
He made me an heir to riches untold
That shall never pass away.

I asked that He would show to me
The path He should decide.
He took my small frail hand in His
And walked close by my side.
I only asked to live with Him
For all eternity,
But a mansion my own in that city fair
He's gone to prepare for me.

I just cannot understand
Why He sought for me one day,
And through His blood on Calvary spilled
Washed my sins away.
My heart is rejoicing since Jesus is mine.
Sin's fetters that once held me fast,
Through Jesus' own blood now lie at my feet
In a broken crumbled mass.

The way may be rough, but His grace is enough
When dark clouds my pathway obscure.
I walk by His side, my father and guide,
And there I'm forever secure.
Tis heaven here with my Jesus near
Though all hell about me rages;
From the raging storms and winds I hide
Safe in the rock of ages

Through It All

Sometimes the storm clouds gather,
And the skies are cloudy and gray;
The path is dark that I travel,
And my feet grow tired on the way.
I can't make the journey without Him
When the path seems dreary and long,
Then I hear the voice of my Savior
Saying, "Be of good courage. Be strong.

I'm walking here beside you.
Nothing can cause you to fall.
The storms, the battle, the burdens,
My grace is sufficient for all.
Look toward the prize set before you.
Keep your eyes on that city so fair.
You will be safe in My keeping
Till you reach your home over there."

Oh what a wonderful promise!
I shall look on His beautiful face.
The tears I have shed here in sorrow
His nail scarred hand will erase.
The journey is almost over.
The race is nearly run.
The battles and trials will seem nothing
When my eyes see the prize I have won.

On The Mountain

I started up the mountain
On a bright and sunny day.
Birds were singing overhead;
Flowers grew along the way.

But soon the air grew colder,
The wind began to blow.
Then the storm clouds gathered
And then the rain and snow.

The climb I thought so easy
Became rough instead,
And the sky above the treetops
Burst in darkness o'er my head.

I trudged slowly up the mountain
Through the rain, the cold, the sleet.
And lo, along the wasteland
Grew some flowers at my feet.

Their faces turned toward heaven
In simple beauty rare,
With colors bright and vivid
Amid the snow flakes there.

No trees grew in that tundra,
Only rock and stone and sand,
But those fragile little flowers
Touched by an unseen hand,

Bloomed in silent beauty,
Bloomed for only God
In that land above the treetops
Where man would seldom trod.

Then my head bowed low in wonder.
The tears fast filled my eyes.
Just God and me alone there
Beneath the cloudless skies.

His love shone all around me.
His presence filled the air,
And I prayed for Him to touch me
Like He touched the flowers there.

I forgot the rugged journey
Through the rain, the cold, the sleet,
When I saw those tiny flowers
Blooming at my feet.

Now if you're climbing through the darkness
From the valley down below,
If your sunshine's turned to showers
And your shower's turned to snow,

Just know that on the mountain
The sun is shining there.
A balmy breeze is blowing.
You can see the flowers fair.

Up above the clouds of darkness,
Up above the sleet and snow,
You will feel God's love surround you
And His blessings fill your soul.

So climb upward, ever upward
Till you stand by grace divine
On the top of that old mountain
In the warmth of God's sunshine.

He's Leading You

Though rough the path and dark the way
That you journey day by day,
Don't forget, when you're sad and blue,
Your Father's hand is leading you.

The thorns that line each weary mile
Will turn to roses after awhile.
The clouds that hang so dark and low
When He sees fit will have to go.

So child of God fresh courage take.
Bear it bravely for His dear sake.
He sees your tears. He hears your prayers.
His heart is burdened with your cares.

The way is rough and dark just now,
But He will bring you out somehow.
So tighten your armor and firmly stand.
Hold tightly to His guiding hand.

Have faith, and cling to Him alone
Whose love can smooth the roughest stone.
Just rest upon His promise true.
Along life's way He's leading you.

In His Control

Hush my soul. Be still and know
O'er every storm God has control.
Through every fierce and stormy gale
His wondrous love will still prevail.
Fear not my soul, there's naught to harm
When sheltered safe neath His loving arm.
Not one wave that dashes high
Is left unseen by the Savior's eye.

Be still my soul. Know even yet
God in heaven won't forget.
But when the way is rough and long
He'll fill the heart with sweetest song.
Rest my soul, nor ever fear.
Nothing can harm when God is near,
Be it stormy seas or winds that blow
All is safe in His control.

And Leave The Rest To Him

God sees the lonely tears that fall
When all the world's asleep.
He knows the treasures of your heart
You've given Him to keep.
He hears the questions you can't ask
When you don't understand,
And he is working for your good
In His eternal plan.
So just keep trusting His great love
In spite of shadows dim.
Hold tightly to His nail scarred hand
And leave the rest to Him.

Leave The Rest To Him

I cannot see the path I walk;
The way just now seems rough.
By faith I'll follow where He leads
Until He says, "Enough."
My heart is burdened down with care.
My eyes with tears are dim.
I'll trust His ever-guiding hand
And leave the rest to Him.

Why need I fear the raging storms?
Why need I worry now?
The problems I don't understand
He'll work them out somehow.
My all-wise Father knows the path.
He'll lead the way that's best,
So I'll just leave it all to Him
And on His promise rest.

Sweetly resting, oh what peace!
I walk close by His side.
Nothing can harm me now,
With Jesus as my guide.
Oh burdened heart bowed down with care
Walking a pathway dim.
Just trust His ever-guiding hand,
And leave the rest to Him.

You Can Find Him In The Shadows

When all is dark around you
And hope seems so in vain,
When your life is filled with sadness,
Your body's filled with pain,
And you can hear no answer
When you call on God in prayer;
Try looking in the shadows.
You'll find Him standing there.

When loved ones have forsaken
And friends are far away,
You can't find one ray of sunshine
To brighten up your day.
When the burdens that you carry
Are just too hard to bear,
It may be in the shadows
That you'll find Him standing there.

Someday this veil of darkness
Will give way to glorious light,
And the dawning of the morning
Will dispel the fears of night.
The heartaches and the sorrow
And the heavy load you bear
Will vanish in a moment
When you see Him standing there.

You Are There

When I walk in crowded places,
You are there.
Searching for familiar faces,
Everywhere.
When I grope along each day,
Trying hard to find my way,
When I have no words to say;
You are there.

When I feel that no one loves me.
You are there.
When the skies are dark above me
Everywhere.
When I'm feeling sad and blue,
Then I catch a glimpse of you,
And I know you'll help me through,
You are there.

When my life is filled with sorrow,
You are there.
Making plans for my tomorrow
Everywhere.
Walking through this troubled land,
Holding to my trembling hand,
Giving grace to help me stand,
You are there.

On The Palm Of His Hand

"Behold I have graven thee on the palm of my hand."
These words, oh how precious to me.
The twilight had fallen, life's way was dark,
So dark that I could not see.
Was there no hope? Had God forgot
His wandering wayward child?
For oh it seemed that I had failed
While walking the long weary mile.

A contrite heart was mine tonight,
One that sought sweet rest.
A soul discouraged seeking a place
Of comfort on Jesus' breast.
Then tearfully I picked up my bible
And secretly whispered a prayer.
"Behold I have graven thee on the palm of my hand."
These words I found written there.

"Can a woman forget her suckling child?
Yes, she may forget," but yet,
'Twas my Savior's voice though discouraged I was,
Telling me He'd never forget.
Others may forsake and turn me aside.
They may not understand,
But I'll rest upon this promise true,
"I have graven thee on the palm of My hand."

I Can Rest

You ask if I grow weary
As I walk the narrow way.
Yes. I grow so weary.
I was weary just today.
But I slipped away alone
From life with all its care
And talked awhile with Jesus
In a secret place of prayer.

As we talked, I heard Him whisper,
"You're tired child, you must rest,"
Then He put his arms around me,
I laid my head upon His breast.
I forgot life's disappointments,
Only knew that He was near.
I was resting—sweetly resting.
His hand had dried each tear.

Oh so often I grow weary
And long for heaven's shore
Where disappointments cannot touch me,
And I'll grow weary never more.
Then I hear my Savior whisper,
"Put your small hand safe in mine.
The hills and rugged mountains
Together we will climb."

Then my feet no longer weary
Press forward in the fight.
For I know that He will lead me
In a path that's always right.
It matters not if I grow weary,
For my Savior knows the best.
He will never, never leave me,
And on His bosom I can rest.

I Love You Daughter

"I love you daughter," He said to me
When the way was rough, no light to see.
"Don't try to walk, but just stand still
That I may show you my perfect will."
So I stood still as He spoke to me,
For the way was dark and I could not see.
Then I saw Him come in victory sweet
To guide with care my trembling feet.

As we walked along, He took my hand.
I'm glad I stood when He said stand.
"I love you daughter," He said to me,
When the way was bright, no clouds to see.
"Let's walk today, just you and I,
Where loved ones fail and friends pass by."
We walked together where the path was dim,
And He drew me tenderly close to Him.

My heart was broken; 'twas a brier-strewn way.
But I'm glad I walked with Him today.
"I love you daughter," He said today.
But I walked alone on the narrow way.
My body was sick with fevered pain.
There was no shelter from the chilling rain.
The way was dark, the mountains steep.
The stones were sharp that pierced my feet.

The burning tears that filled my eyes
Only hid from view the sunlit skies.
But then He came and walked with me,
And it mattered not that I could not see.
We often walk, just He and I,
Where loved fail and friends pass by.
Where chilly rains and winds that blow
Would harm for ere my ransomed soul;

Where raging storms would mar His grace,
And darkened clouds would hide His face.
But all of these can never harm
When sheltered safe neath His loving arms.
With Him beside me every day
I'd rather walk a brier-strewn way.
Of peace and joy naught can compare.
When Jesus walks beside me there.

Look Toward The Sunrise

When your soul is sad within you,
Bowed with toil and care,
Look toward the sunrise.
You'll find God's presence there.
And as your eyes behold it,
You'll see His hand of love
Caress the brow of heaven
From his kingdom up above.
If you would see God's glory,
Just keep your gaze on high.
As His fingers brush the colors
On the canvas of the sky,
So His hand of love will touch you
And brush your cares away.
If you'll look toward the sunrise,
You can face the coming day.

The Road of Life

Life's road is swiftly winding
Down the path of time.
It's stamping deep its image
Upon your heart and mine.
Though our one sure goal is heaven,
Many lessons we must learn
From the all wise God, our maker,
Ere our soul to Him return.

There are separate roads we travel,
For planned within His will
Is a separate place of duty
For each child of His to fill.
And the path that is your portion
May lead through sorrow's door.
Do not question; only follow.
He has walked this way before.

God desired the purest vessel,
One all broken, tender, true
To bear salvation's story,
And He has chosen you
You may suffer grief and sorrow.
Your heart may broken be,
For He would mold a perfect vessel
For all the world to see.

Many lives have tasted sorrow.
Broken hearts are crushed with pain.
You're His child. He loves you dearly.
You must reap the golden grain.
Wait patiently. The prayers you've uttered
Are recorded up on high.
He sees the tears of sorrow
As you kneel alone to cry.

He knows your heart is broken.
He hears you from His throne,
And of His riches up in glory
You've a portion all your own.
There's a day, and soon its coming,
Though the path just now is rough,
When He'll stay the hand of Satan,
And say, "It is enough."

Life's Battlefield

I feel almost like an old warrior tonight.
The battle is waging hard.
My soul is weary from fighting long.
My hands and feet are all scarred.
But there's victory ahead. I can see through the dim
My captain is leading the way.
So I'll tighten my armor and fight close to Him.
Fight till the close of the day.

My strength's almost gone and courage near spent,
But my captain is speaking to me.
His voice through the din of the battle I hear,
"My grace is sufficient for thee."
I'll fight by His side through the heat of the day.
I'll fight through the dark of the night.
I'll fight till the battle is over and won
And the foe has taken his flight.

Soon twilight will fall and the evening
Bid farewell to life's short day,
And I'll stand on that great battlefield of time
Where the dead and the wounded lay.
Lord, thou who art my captain
Help me fight till the set of life's sun,
Till the warfare of life is ended
And the battle is over and won.

The Master Weaver

As your journey on toward Heaven,
You are weaving every day.
And the pattern will be finished
At the ending of the way.
Jesus is the Master weaver;
For your life a plan He'll choose.
He holds within His keeping
All the colors you may use.

When the threads of life get tangled
From the work you've tried to do,
Give the broken threads to Jesus.
Let Him weave them all for you.
He's the One who holds the pattern.
He's the master weaver true,
And life's threads will never tangle
If you let Him work for you.

When your weaving is completed,
And you put your work away,
You will see the Master weaver
At the closing of life's day.
So weave a perfect pattern
With the purples, blues, and golds
That your work will match completely
With the pattern that He holds.

Jesus Cares

I'm glad that Jesus cares
When trials press me sore,
When burdens make the pathway rough,
And shadows gather o'er.
To think that he would hover near
When the way is rough and steep,
Fill my heart with gladness,
And guide my trembling feet.

I'm glad that Jesus cares.
With His strong and loving arm
He gathers me close to His bosom,
And shelters me from all harm.
His presence goes before me.
His love lights the darkest day.
With His nail scarred hand He leads me
Each step along the way.

Oh I'm glad that Jesus cares.
With my head upon His breast,
He whispers that He loves me,
Gives me grace for every test.
There's no path too rough to follow.
He my every burden bears.
Not a cross to hard to carry
When I know that Jesus cares

I Will Fight For You

Stand still my child. Don't struggle long
O'er battles fierce and words said wrong.
Don't heed at all the mocking throng,
But through the test be true.

The battles hard you need not fight,
But trust in Me with all your might,
And everything will be alright.
I will fight for you.

The fiercest battle is not so hard.
Just rest awhile if you're from it scarred,
And victory will be your reward
When I fight for you.

Weep no more oh trembling soul
O'er storms so fierce and winds that blow.
Remember I still have control,
And I will still the storm.

In the night I'll give a song.
In your weakest moment I am strong.
I will keep you from all wrong
'Neath my sheltering arm.

Trust in Me, nor question why.
I've seen the tears and heard your cry,
And I will answer by and by.
When I think best.

The mountains may be hard to climb,
But my clock above keeps perfect time,
Not too fast and not behind,
So on My promise rest.

The dark clouds now my face may hide.
Oh troubled soul I'm by your side.
Remember that my hand doth guide,
So through the test be true.

Just wait awhile. Don't struggle now.
Before my throne just humbly bow,
And I will work it out somehow.
I will see you through.

The Narrow Road

They tell me the way is narrow
And filled with many a stone.
They say there are thorns on the pathway,
And I'll have to travel alone.
They tell me the sun never shines there,
The skies are cloudy and gray.
They warn me not to walk there,
For many have fallen by the way.

But they see only the thorns,
While I see the roses so bright.
I can see the sunshine,
While they see only the night.
The road is rough and narrow.
It is filled with many a stone,
And thorns do line its pathway,
But I don't walk it alone.

For Jesus walks beside me,
And if I feel it's all in vain
When I stumble and fall in the dusty road
He helps me up again.
I stand upon His promise
And He helps me through each test.
He's with me when I'm tempted
And helps me do my best.

Miscellaneous

I will praise thee, O LORD,
with my whole heart;
I will show forth all
thy marvelous works.
I will be glad and rejoice
in thee: I will sing
praise to thy name,
O thou most high.

Psalm 9:1 - 2 (KJV)

When Jesus Touched Me

I'll never forget the day that Jesus touched me,
When as a little child I knelt to pray.
I never dreamed that He could love me.
For He always seemed to be so far away.
But in my heart, I wished that I could see Him,
And as I watched the clouds up in the sky,
I wondered if He knew how much I loved Him,
And if He noticed when I slipped away to cry.

I wondered if He knew I'd like to know him
And have Him lay his hand upon my head
Like He did those little children in the Bible
Who gathered close to hear the words He said.
Then one day all alone He stood beside me
And spoke my name just like I wished He would.
He whispered softly that He loved me,
And deep inside I knew He understood.

Then my heart reached out in faith and touched Him.
He drew me close to Him that day.
And somehow I knew He'd always been there,
Even when He seemed so far away.
And just like those little children in the Bible
Who gathered there to hear the words He said,
In marvelous love I know that Jesus touched me,
I felt Him lay His hand upon my head.

Since that day He walks along beside me
In the sunshine or in the twilight dim,
For with that touch, He changed me so completely.
I've never been the same since I met Him.
And someday when this life is over,
And the sky above is rolled back like a scroll
I'll no longer watch those clouds and think of Jesus.
I'll no longer feel that longing in my soul.

For in the twinkling of an eye, I'll go to meet Him
Far above this world with all its care
To a land of love that lies beyond the river.
An angel choir will welcome me up there.
Then face to face I know that I shall see Him,
And from this robe of flesh I shall be free.
To walk with Him upon those streets of glory
And live with Him through all eternity

The Lowly Nazarene

I walked alone one summer day
Down a long and dusty road.
My heart was bowed in deep despair
With sin's great heavy load.
When in the distance there I saw
A quiet peaceful scene:
A stately church standing tall
Upon a mound of green.

I stepped inside those stately doors.
A quiet hush was there,
As the sweet old songs the organ played
Flowed out upon the air.
I sat upon a cushioned pew,
And the choir began to sing.
The summer sunlight danced and played
On the stained glass window pane.

The song the choir sang was good,
Their voices sweet and clear,
But it didn't touch my troubled heart
Or calm my doubt and fear.
I saw no blessed Son of God,
No cross of Calvary,
No Savior stood with outstretched arms
In love to pardon me.

I left, my heart was heavy,
Still bowed in deep despair.
I carried now a greater load
Than when I entered there.
'Twas a grand old church I saw that day
On that little mound of green,
But within its doors I found no trace
Of the Lowly Nazarene.

I walked again another day
Down a long and dusty road.
My heart was bowed near to despair
By sin's great heavy load.
When in the distance there I saw
A quiet peaceful scene:
A stately church standing tall
Upon a mound of green.

A quiet hush fell on my soul
As I stepped inside the door.
I sensed a gentle presence there
I'd never felt before.
I sat upon a cushioned pew.
The organ softly played.
The people sang a sweet old song,
And then they knelt and prayed.

Then the choir rose to sing
As tears rolled down each face.
With voices touched with Heaven's glow
They sang "Amazing Grace."
I saw the blessed Son of God.
I saw Mount Calvary.
From the middle cross upon a hill
A Savior beckoned me.

And as the tears rolled down my face,
I saw the price He paid.
With burdened heart and troubled soul
I bowed my head and prayed.
Many years have come and gone,
And that old church on the hill
Is there no more. The choir song
Is now forever still.

But the peace and joy I found that day
Have lasted through the years
To keep me steady through the storms
And calm my doubts and fears.
And I'll never forget that stately church
That long past summer day,
With stained glass windows and cushioned pews
Where first I knelt to pray.

It stands a symbol in my heart
Of a straight and narrow way,
Where now I walk with God alone,
Of night changed into day.
I thank God for love and heaven,
For peace and joy supreme
For that grand old church where first I met
The lowly Nazarene.

It matters not where we may sit,
On wood or cushioned pew.
It matters not if the glass is stained,
Or lets the sunshine through.
It matters not if the choir is robed,
Their voices trained and true,
If there are thousands gathered there
Or just a faithful few.

It need not be a stately church
With carpet on the floor.
What matters most is what is felt
When one walks through the door.
It's always good to feel the hush
Of a quiet peaceful scene,
But it's better far to feel the touch
Of the lowly Nazarene.

Tell Them

Her hair was spiked and dyed a purple hue.
Paint streaked black around her eyes of blue.
Seeking for something to give her peace
And make the ache inside of her to cease.
Tell her she is seeking for Me.

Standing on the corner trying not to fall,
Bleary-eyed he smiled at everyone he saw,
Seeking to satisfy the aching void within,
To free him from the guilt of past committed sin.
Tell him he is seeking for Me.

Lying in a stupor in a hovel dank and dim,
The needle used to inject the drug still lying close to him.
The only way he knew to make his sorrow go away
Was to pass into oblivion day after day.
Tell him he is seeking for Me

She never would have done it if she had only known,
Before she killed her unborn child, that she'd feel so alone.
Sitting in a tavern, staring into space,
Seeking for something to free her from disgrace.
Tell her she is seeking for Me.

Booze and tears co-mingled with the vomit on the floor.
He'd had his fill of a sinful life, and yet he longed for more,
He'd tried in vain to free him from the wine, booze and dope,
And now at last alone and lost, he'd given up all hope.
Tell him he is seeking for Me.

People all around us; each day they pass us by.
We hug the secret to our heart, ignore their anxious cry.
And all the while a Savior is pleading from above
"I want to set them free, but they don't know about My love.
Tell them-tell them they are seeking for Me."

Through Eyes of Love

I passed an old man on the street,
With trembling hand and shuffling feet.
His head was bowed in deep despair.
I passed him by and left him there.

I heard the blind man's weak demand,
An empty tin cup in his hand.
I turned my head and went away,
Nor thought of him again that day.

I saw a stranger bent with care,
With tattered garments and tangled hair.
With tear filled eyes, she looked at me,
But I didn't heed her silent plea.

I knelt that night beside my bed,
Folded my hands and bowed my head,
Lifted my eyes toward the skies above;
"Lord help me see through your eyes of love"

I walked again another day
A little slower on my way.
As if in answer to my prayer,
That day I saw no strangers there.

I saw my father on the street
With trembling hand and shuffling feet.
I walked and talked with him a while,
And when I left, I saw him smile.

I saw my brother sitting there,
A white tipped cane beside his chair.
I gave to him a larger cup,
And to the brim I filled it up.

I passed a stranger, and in her place,
I saw my sister's weeping face.
And to my heart I drew her near,
Gave her all I had and calmed her fear.

I saw my mother bent and gray
Going on her lonely way.
In my heart I heard her silent plea,
Then I took her home with me.

And so the people that we meet
Are not just strangers on the street,
But someone's sister, someone's brother,
Son or daughter, father, mother.

So don't go heedlessly rushing by.
Take time to hear their anxious cry,
And you will find that in their place,
You'll see the Savior's smiling face.

His Hands

His hands, rough, scarred,
The hands of a carpenter.
Smoothing the rough edges,
Fitting together the pieces,
Making something beautiful
Of the wood.

His hands, gentle, nail scarred,
The hands of a Savior.
Smoothing the rough places,
Fitting together the broken pieces,
Making something beautiful
Of my life.

Five Loaves And Two Small Fishes

Just five loaves and two small fishes
Was all he had.
Not much to feed five thousand,
Not much to feed a lad.

He carried it gently saving it
For when the day was spent.
He kicked the pebbles on the road,
Whistling as he went.

With dusty feet and sweating brow,
He reached his destiny,
Pushing shoving through the crowd
To see what he could see.

At last he reached a clearing
And sat upon the ground.
Jesus stood a way apart,
His disciples gathered 'round.

For hours he sat and listened,
A simple bare foot boy.
The words the Master spoke that day
Filled his heart with joy.

He felt the pangs of hunger
When the day was hot and long.
And he longed to eat his home-made lunch
As he eyed the dusty throng.

Then he felt a nudge and heard a voice,
Speak through the restless dim.
"The Master needs just what you have.
Will you give your lunch to Him?"

A quiet hush fell on the crowd.
The youngster bowed his head.
He eyed his five small fishes
And his two loaves of bread.

Then he saw the Master look
Through eyes care worn and dim.
He slowly lifted up his lunch
And held it out to Him.

Lord, I can't feed the thousands
With my limited supply.
The small amount of crumbs I have
Won't feed the passers by.

But take my loaves and fishes, Lord.
It isn't much I know.
Use them to bless the hungry hearts
As you did so long ago.

Unworthy of Him

I know I'm the least of God's children,
Of all who partake of His grace.
I bowed low at His feet one night,
Unworthy to look on His face.
My heart with sin's burden was heavy.
My eyes with tears were dim.
He lifted the load that crushed me,
And bade me to follow Him.

I know I'm the least of God's children.
Oft I've marveled how it could be
That God's own son in heaven loves me,
From every sin He sets me free.
And often I wonder just what He saw
That night in the twilight dim,
When He took me in His loving arms
And gathered me close to Him.

Oh I know I'm the least of God's children,
And I can't quite understand
Why He leads me through the dark valleys
With His own dear nail scarred hand.
My finite mind can't grasp it,
And often I wonder why
He takes time out to talk with me
And listen when I cry.

My heart cries out in the stillness
As I think of the love He gave.
"I'm not worthy to be a hired servant.
Oh just let me be a love slave."
Though I toil from dawn until evening
For souls who are lost in the night,
Yet the cross that I bear is not heavy,
For love makes the burden light

I know when the shadows gather,
And the daytime fades away,
Though I've given my all to His keeping,
The debt I can never repay.
Yes, I'm the least of God's children,
And when life's sun forever grows dim,
And I've done for the last time His bidding,
I'll still be unworthy of Him.

The Pattern

I decided one day to make a dress.
I knew that I could do it.
I needed no one to tell me how.
There was really nothing to it.

I cut the pieces carefully,
And sewed them one by one.
It didn't take much time
To get the garment done.

But alas! My finished work
Didn't look much like a dress.
I knew that I'd done something wrong.
It really was a mess.

One place was much too big
Another much too small.
It didn't even look quite right,
And it just didn't fit at all.

I knew I'd cut the pattern right
And used the right size thread,
But I thought about the instructions
I hadn't even read.

I made another garment.
I made it carefully.
I read all the instructions
And followed them to a Tee.

And I don't need to tell you
When at long last I was through,
This one looked much better,
And fit much better too.

Our life is like a garment
We each set out to sew.
We have a book of instructions
With all we need to know.

How many times we fail to read
What the Master has to say.
Life is nothing but a mess
When we do things our own way.

We must give to God the pieces
Of our troubled sin sick soul,
For He knows just exactly
Where each piece should go.

He holds fast the pattern
To each life within His hand,
And He will fit the pieces
According to His plan.

The Church And The World

The church and the world walked along one day,
And each walked alone upon life's way;
The church pure and holy by sin undefiled,
The world proud and haughty by sin made wild.
The world looked on at the church in her place,
And trembled in fear as he thought of her grace.
For the church pure and holy in every day life
Defied all the world with its sin and strife.

The church and the world walked along one day,
And the church toward the world began to stray.
The world looked on in great surprise
When he saw the church wink her eyes.
The world remembered the church true and pure,
And thought that he must be mistaken sure.
Thus the world traveled on in great surprise
At the thought that the church had winked her eyes.

The church and the world walked along life's road,
But the church had lost its joys untold.
The glory of God no more shone through;
The church no longer was pure and true.
The world no more would tremble with fear,
For he knew that God was no longer near.
The church and the world walked side by side,
And the church was haughty and filled with pride.

The church and the world walk along each day
Now hand in hand along life's way.
And the poor old world oft laughs low
At the church and the way she has chosen to go.
When someday before God the church will stand,
Will the blood of the world be upon her hands,
Since from God and holiness and the narrow way
In her folly and pride she turned one day?

And will some mother's child sink in hell,
Because the church in her folly no more can tell
The way of salvation she used to know
Before she turned her feet with the world to go?
Will it by my child unprepared
Who stands before God and cries to be spared?
Will I with the church once holy stand
While the blood of my child drips from my hand?

Oh church in your folly sin and shame
Seek not the pleasures of worldly fame.
Turn from your sin and foolish pride
To walk once again with the crucified.
Let the world in its wickedness sin and strife
Again walk alone down the path of life.
Then the world in its sin will lose its allure
And tremble once more at the church true and pure.

The Lovely Flower

While walking through life's garden
Alone one busy day,
I spied a lovely flower
That grew along the way.
Its stem was straight and sturdy,
Its petals pure and fair;
And I thought it was the fairest
Of the flowers blooming there.

I said, "It soon will wither,
And soon it will decay.
Like all the other flowers,
It soon will fade away."
For years I walked life's garden.
For years I watched it grow.
Its leaves stayed fresh and pretty.
Its petals pure as snow.

And my heart was filled with wonder.
The flower still blooming there
For years had never withered,
Only grown more pure and fair.
I saw the storm clouds gather.
I saw the rain drops start
And beat upon that flower.
I watched with fearful heart.

I watched the storm clouds scatter,
The rain drops cease to fall.
But lo! The lovely flower stood
Still fairer than them all.
Then my heart rejoiced in silence,
And my load much lighter grew,
As I gazed spell bound with wonder
At the flower still standing true.

And no doubt many a traveler,
Who walks life's dusty way,
Remembers this lovely flower
As he journeys day by day.
Oh I pray that God will keep her
Always pure and true,
For this flower fair and lovely
Dear saint of God is you.

Satan's Junkyard

One day while sore discouraged
I wandered sad and lone,
When suddenly I saw these words
Engraved upon a stone:
"Satan's Junk Yard," Its letters bright
Caused me to pause a while.
With curious heart I stepped inside
To search it, every mile.

Suddenly through the mist I saw
On a sign in letters bold,
"Here are weapons for backsliding
That have proved useless and old."
To my surprise I saw before me
A furnace hot and vast.
Why it must be the one in which
The three Hebrews were cast.

'Twas thrown in Satan's junk yard
Up on an old trash pile.
To know the reason why just then,
I had to think a while.
Then suddenly to my pondering mind
I recalled the story old:
Though God's children were tried in fire,
They had come forth as gold.

Oh the things I saw as then I searched
Satan's junk yard through and through.
To my surprise the ground was covered
With junk that had proven untrue:
Silver and gold all scattered about
And a den of lions too,
False tales and false doctrines.
All of these had proven untrue.

There were trials and temptations,
Tattle wagons galore,
Boxes of deceitfulness
All scattered on the floor.
There were giants huge and powerful,
And heavy crosses there,
Homes and bears and lions
And burdens hard to bear.

There were lies and lies and more lies
Confusions, darkness, and ills,
Gossipers and talebearers
With tongues that were used to kill.
And oh there were doubts and fears I know
That covered nearly a mile,
And so much more I cannot tell,
For I stunned a while.

There I was sore discouraged
With all that junk scattered about,
When discouragement was just another weapon
That Satan was trying out.
So let's overcome discouragement,
And when the day of testing is passed,
Satan another weapon
Into his junk yard must cast.

My Own Big Brother

Just a bit of sunshine
Scattered along my way.
A friendly smile, a kindly word
To make complete each day.

I cannot quite explain it.
I may laugh sometimes, it's true,
At the silly little things you say
And the funny things you do.

But deep down inside my heart,
I guess I must admit,
In spite of all you do and say,
I really think you're it.

And of all the friends I chance to meet
There will surely be no other
Who'll ever really quite compare
To my own big brother.

Life's Song

Life is a song you are singing.
Each note has been chosen with care
By the hand of the Master Composer,
Sent on the wings of a prayer.

Your voice will blend to perfection
If you follow the music just so
And sing every note as it's written,
Never too fast or too slow.

And if for a time there is silence
That seemingly never will end,
Then rest-and wait for the signal
Before you start singing again.

Don't sing too loud or too softly.
Take care to miss not a beat
If you want your song to be perfect
When your time for singing's complete.

Life's Gateway

I entered a beautiful gateway
While traveling one day on life's road.
The pathway was strewn with flowers
That seemed to be tinted with gold.
Birds sang a song from the treetops
That reached out their arms to the sky
And beckoned the weary old sunshine
To smile on those who pass by.

I journeyed for days on this pathway,
And I longed to rest a while,
For the way was dusty, and the sunshine
Had lost its enticing smile.
But the road led on at a downward pace;
No shade could I find by the way.
The flowers were fading, and the song of the birds
No longer seemed happy and gay.

This road had a beautiful gateway,
But I found to my dismay
The path I journeyed would not lead home,
Only farther and farther away.
There's many a gateway on the road of life
That beckons the young and the old
To enter and seek for the fortune and fame
That awaits at the end of the road.

And many a lovely pathway
Is filled with bitter strife.
But there's only one way to follow
That leads to eternal life.
And you who are traveling life's path
No matter how far you may roam,
Be sure that you enter the gateway
That leads to your heavenly home.

The Judgment

I dreamed I stood at the Judgment,
Stood with the multitude there
Awaiting an entrance to heaven,
That city so bright and so fair.

As I glanced o'er the vast crowd that waited
On the faces of some that I knew,
I wondered, because of the life they'd lived,
Just how they could make it through.

For some had scolded, and some found fault.
Some did things I just couldn't do.
Something was wrong with each of them;
They were hypocrites I knew.

And so I stood there finding fault
As each one stood before God,
Picking out only the wrong things I'd seen
As life's pathway they had trod.

Soon it was my turn to stand before my maker
To be judged by God on high.
Trembling and helpless I stood before Him
Who had created earth and sky.

And quickly I began to tell of the others
And all the faults I thought they had,
How those who should have been spotless
In dirty robes were clad.

But He spoke to me so gently,
"Tis not so child, in my sight
Those robes you've judged to be dirty
Are spotless and pure and white.

Then I looked at my own robe so proudly
Feeling sure I too would enter in,
But lo! My robe was spotted and dirty
And stained with the marks of sin.

Was it True! Could I have been so busy
Finding fault because these were not right
That my own robe had grown dingy and dirty,
No more so pure and white?

For my robe has lost all its brightness.
No more did it shine forth as new.
I had only found fault with others,
Nor tried to help them through.

I could not bear to lift my eyes
To the piercing eyes of God,
For He seemed to see into my heart;
Seemed to know the path I'd trod.

"Lord forgive," I cried, but I awoke just then
And fell to my knees in prayer.
No more to find fault with others,
But only their burdens share.

That my robe may gain its brightness,
And once more shine forth as new,
Not finding fault with others,
But helping them make it through.

So Shall His Coming Be

The lightning flashed across the dark dense sky.
The thunder roared; a storm was nigh.
I read God's word, my heart filled with fear,
When suddenly a voice whispered in my ear.
"For as the lightning did flash you see,
So shall the coming of the Son of Man be."
"O how quickly," I cried. In the twinkling of an eye
The lightning had flashed across the dark, dense sky.
No time to think, not even to pray.
In one second it flashed, then went away.
In one second so bright every eye could see.
So shall the coming of the Son of Man be.
Never before had I thought it that way;
No time to think, not even to pray.
No time for idle words as we run this race.
We've only time to seek the Master's face.
For as the lightning flashed you see,
So shall the coming of the Son of Man be.

The Invitation

I received an invitation
In the mail today.
"You're invited to a wedding
On the twenty-third of May."
My heart was filled with gladness.
I wanted to attend,
For it was the invitation
To the wedding of a friend.

I made my plans rejoicing,
Had things fixed up just so,
And as that day approached,
I could hardly wait to go.
I washed and cleaned each garment
With tender loving care.
I had chosen them so carefully,
The clothes that I would wear.

For I wanted to look lovely,
Spotless, bright and clean,
And I wanted to be perfect,
Not a blemish to be seen.
But alas! My plans changed quickly.
My heart was filled with woe,
For to my disappointment,
I found I could not go.

I thought about another day
When God in His great love
Sent me an invitation
To a marriage feast above.
And my heart sent back an answer,
"I have started on my way
To that last great wedding supper
On that grand and glorious day."

I've exchanged sin's tattered garments
For a robe of beauty rare,
A spotless robe, the Bridegroom sent,
That He wanted me to wear.
I am making plans rejoicing.
I want everything just so,
And as that day approaches,
I can hardly wait to go.

I am careful every moment
From dawn till day is done,
For I don't want to miss
The wedding of God's son.
Then I'll meet my soul's true lover,
Walk forever by His side,
For at that last great marriage supper,
I intend to be the bride.

Faith Is

Faith is believing when there is no hope,
Loving when you cannot feel,
Putting your hand in an unseen hand
And knowing God is real.

Faith is seeing what you cannot see
And hearing what you cannot hear.
Faith is walking where there is no path
And knowing God is near.

Faith is trusting when it makes no sense
Whether it be good or ill.
Faith is knowing that whatever comes,
It is God's perfect will.

There Is A Way Through

There is a way through, though dark be the valley
And rugged the path to that shore.
There is a way through; it's merely by following
In the footsteps of one gone before.
The stones may be rough that pierce our feet
Till we think we cannot stand.
But there is a way through, though we cannot see it.
It's only by holding to His nail scarred hand.

The hills may be steep as onward we journey,
And we feel we must rest by the way.
But there's one who beside us will comfort and guide us
And give us strength as our day.
There is a way through; it's just to press onward,
Not looking behind us one minute,
Till clouds pass away and a sweet voice whispers,
"Child this the way, walk ye in it."

There is a way through, and they surely will find it
Who, in a secret place of prayer
Await the answer God has promised
To those who tarry with Him there.
For every valley shall be exalted.
Each mountain and hill be made low.
The rough shall be plain, the crooked straight.
He has spoken, and it shall be so

There is a way through. No power of Satan
Can ever withstand his great love,
Who watches o'er his dear children
And points out the way from above.
Oh glorious the thought; naught can stop us
On our journey to heaven's fair land.
There is a way through, It's just to press onward
And hold to His nail scarred hand.

Tomorrow

The clouds will lift tomorrow that mar my path today.
If I will walk with Jesus, He'll lead me all the way.
The shadows soon will scatter, although it seems in vain,
If I will trust In Jesus, the sun will shine again.

I'll feel His presence near me, though it may be after while,
Because I know He's walking beside me every mile.
His hand's still holding my hand, though I cannot touch him now,
If I rest upon His promise, He'll work it out somehow.

He's coming soon from glory, though I cannot see Him yet.
He's promised a home in heaven, and He will not forget.
So if you've grown discouraged, just put your trust in Him,
And when the storms are over, the sun will shine again.

Trust fully in His leading. Question not nor fear.
The one who knows the future will make the pathway clear.
Rest securely in His keeping, though you cannot see it now,
The one who sees from heaven will work it out somehow

I Know My Guide

I may not know the future or what lies ahead for me.
There may be many dangers that now I do not see.
There may be many pitfalls ahead on life's great road,
Persecutions, tests and trials, or many a heavy load.

I may not know the future, but I have a friend who knows,
One who walks beside me and conquers all my foes,
One who holds my hand in His and stays close by my side.
No, I do not know the future, but I know full well my guide.

He's Jesus, the Son of God who's walked this way before.
It matters not that I am tired and tested o'er and o'er.
For in the hour of persecution He stays near by my side.
I don't need to know the future, because I know my guide.

He will not lead me wrong. He'll hold tightly to my hand,
And when I'm tested and tried, He'll help me to understand.
He will let not me stray from Him; He's always by my side.
I don't want to know the future, I'll just trust it to my guide.

Our Father

There is a God in heaven
Who belongs to you and me.
He is our Heavenly Father.
We're His children, don't you see.

He never, never slumbers,
But watches night and day
Over all His precious children
Who walk the narrow way.

His ear is ever listening.
Not one word He does not hear
When He meets His own dear children
In a secret place of prayer.

He knows our deep desires,
And He sees the tears that fall.
He understands our every need
And supplies them one and all.

My heart overflows with gladness.
I cannot fathom how could be.
God in Heaven is our Father.
We're His children, you and me.

We Can Trust Our Heavenly Father

When the sun shone in my world,
All was calm and still,
And o'er the air sweet music flowed
From the song of the Whippoorwill.

I said, "My heavenly Father
Has planned this all for me."
And I reveled in the beauty
As far as my eye could see.

Then the sun faded into darkness,
Clouds gathered overhead,
And all was still-the Whippoorwill
Was lying cold and dead.

Then I looked up to heaven
Through eyes with tears made dim,
And said, "It is my Father's will.
I'll still sing praise to Him.

My loving Heavenly Father
Has planned this all for me.
And I will trust His planning
Even though I cannot see."

Could it be our Heavenly Father
In His wisdom and His love
Sends the sunshine and the shadows
From His kingdom up above?

And both are filled with beauty.
And both bring peace and rest.
We can trust our Heavenly Father
To always know what's best

When God Says It's Enough

When God say it's enough,
The storm-clouds have to flee.
The skies of gray must go away;
They cannot trouble me.
Though Satan tries my faith to shake
I know that God will not forsake.
When storms along my pathway sweep,
I know that God has power to keep.

When God says it's enough
The powers of darkness go.
The God I love sends from above
An anchor for my soul.
Though Satan tries his best to prove
That God can't hills and mountains move,
Just one small touch of His great hand
Makes flowers bloom in desert sand.

And He will move in His own time
The mountains that are hard to climb.
Superior man can hold no sway
O'er blessings that would come my way,
For God is greater yet by far
Than men in high positions are.
Just one small thought from His great mind
Could put an end to all mankind.

The powers of darkness have to go
That dim the sunlight of my soul.
The cloud of doubt and dread and fear
Give way to faith and hope and cheer.
So I'll walk each day with my hand in His,
Though dark the path and rough.
His light across my path will shine
When God says it's enough.

He's My Father; I'm His Child

The storm about me rages
On the troubled sea of life.
The wind in fury blows
And fills my heart with strife.
But there's One who sees from heaven
The storms that blow so wild.
I know they cannot harm me,
He's my Father, I'm His child.

It's a troubled sea I'm sailing,
And the breakers dash and toss
Till it seems that through the tempest
My soul will soon be lost.
But there is a voice from heaven,
Speaks to calm the raging wild,
Holds me fast within His keeping;
He's my Father. I'm His child

Oh the storms can never harm me
Nor the fearful winds that blow.
My Father sees from Heaven
And guards my ransomed soul.
Safe am I within His keeping
From the storms that rage so wild,
Safe from every dashing billow;
He's my Father. I'm His child.

God Is There

In the evening's fading light,
In the darkness of the night,
Midst the battles that we fight,
God is there.

When the way is long and drear,
When we've lost a loved one dear,
When our heart is filled with fear,
God is there.

When everything's all right,
When we climb the mountain height,
When the sun is shining bright
God is there,

God's Abiding Love

Softly the shades of nighttime
Descend upon the day,
Causing the lingering shadows
To silently slip away.
I open my heart to the stillness,
Lift my eyes above,
And feel the calm assurance
Of God's abiding love

My Soul's True Lover

He is not here - only a longing
Fills my heart and makes me weep.
He is gone, my soul's true lover.
There's only a pathway rough and steep.

My heart has searched for His presence.
My soul has cried in despair;
Cried for my heart's true lover,
Only to find He is not there.

Behold I go backward and forward.
I search to the left, to the right,
Search for my soul's true lover
Only to find one long dark night.

Will He never again come to me?
My heart says " It is not so."
I know He'll come,
Though the clouds hang dark and low

He will come because He loves me.
He'll take me in His arms again,
Draw me up close to His bosom
And shelter me there from the rain.

He is here! Gone is the longing
That once filled my heart with distress.
He is here, my soul's true lover,
And safe in His keeping I rest .

My Father Cares

I was lonely one day. God sent a friend
The lonely hours with me to spend.
I was tired one day from traveling long.
He gave me rest, filled my heart with song.
I was burdened one day along life's road.
He walked beside me, helped to bear my load.
Dark clouds one day across the sky were lined.
He chased them away, made the sun to shine.

I was sick one day with fevered pain.
One touch of His hand made me well again.
I was in need one day of earthly store.
He supplied my need, then gave me more.
My heavenly Father cares for me,
Supplies my need whatere it be.
No mortal tongue can ere impart.
My Father grants the desires of my heart

Such As I

When I was but a little child
In days not long ago,
I used to wish that Christ would walk
Once again down here below.
I used to wish He'd take my hand
And lead me all the while.
I often wished to hear Him speak
And longed to see Him smile.

But I didn't think He'd really walk
Life's dusty way so drear,
And I didn't think He'd really speak
So that such as I could hear.
But there came a day as years went on
That my heart once learned to seek,
And through the stillness of the night
I heard my Savior speak.

I didn't think He'd really take
My frail hand in His so strong,
Guide me through a world of sin
And keep me from all wrong.
But I find He really walks with me
And leads me all the while.
When sorrow and heartaches gather near
Through my tears I see Him smile.

I used to think, when but a child,
That Jesus lived way up in the sky,
With no thought at all for earthly care,
Far away from such as I.
But I often think about it now,
And oft times the tears will start,
When I think how the great big God above
Abides within my heart.

I used to think that the mansions
He's gone to prepare for His own
Would be for the great, the noble and true
As they gather around His throne.
But oh to think that He has made
One such as I an heir
To a mansion up in glory
He has gone himself to prepare.

I used to think about Him coming back,
And I wondered if one like me
Could someday life with Jesus
Through all eternity.
But since the night He spoke to me
And saved me by His grace,
I know that someday even I
Shall see Him face to face.

The Golden Morn

God gave me a friend one day.
I knew it not then.
The sky was a glorious golden hue,
A rainbow of fairest blend.
But twilight came and with it the clouds.
The skies above turned gray,
And I wept, for my heart in silence longed
For the rainbow of yesterday.
But the darkened sky only laughed and mocked.
The wind only echoed its scorn.
And my heart shuddered, and cried and wept
And wished for the golden morn.
But the storm beat fierce; the wind blew wild
And dashed my troubled soul.
I longed and begged and cried for light,
Just a tiny golden glow.
Then morning came, and light, I thought.
As I lay on the shifting sand,
For through the dark and stormy night
You gave to me your hand.
My heart cried loud, as I turned to look,
And beheld your weeping eyes.
For there was no brightness of the morning sun,
Only dark and stormy skies.
Your heart too was bent with care
And crushed with bitter pain.
Together we stood on the shifting sand,
And faced the chilling rain.
The wind only blew more swift and fierce.
The sky only darker grew.
The clouds only laughed and mocked and scorned
And hid the golden hue.

The billows dashed our troubled souls,
And then I realized,
You too, had longed and begged and wept
For yesterday's golden skies.
Together we stood and faced the storm,
And our faith much stronger grew.
The storms and clouds and darkened skies
Gave place to the golden hue.
And morning came, and with it the light,
No longer to beg and pray.
Its glorious beauty so far excelled
The rainbow of yesterday.
And thus we stand on life's great shore
And face its storm swept sea
With none but Jesus ever near,
Our pilot and friend to be.
Soon earth's storms will all be over.
We'll come to the end of life's way,
And eternity's morn will far exceed
The rainbow we see today.

The Old Earthen Vessel

They tell me an old earthen vessel
Once lay by the wayside alone.
So dirty and dingy, so ugly
And useless it lay midst the stones.
The people passed by and shook their head
When the old earthen vessel they saw,
And sadly said it would never
Be of much use at all.

A kind old man passed by one day
And looked at the vessel there.
He saw far beyond its being of clay,
A thing of beauty rare.
He planted a tiny little seed
Within the vessel of clay,
And he tended with care until it grew
Into a lovely flower one day.

The people passed by and gazed in awe
At the flower so lovely and fair.
So great was its beauty, the people scarce knew
The old earthen vessel was there.
And may I like that old earthen vessel
Live each day with His presence near,
And be filled with His Spirit till the people scarce know
This old earthen vessel is here.

Come Walk In My Garden

Though the fig tree may not blossom,
nor fruit be on the vines;
though the labor of the olive may fail,
and the fields yield no food;
though the flock may be cut off from the fold,
and there be no herd in the stalls -
Yet I will rejoice in the Lord,
I will joy in the God of my salvation.

Habakkuk 3:17 - 18 (NIV)

Come Walk In My Garden

Come walk in my garden where balmy breezes blow,
Birds sing in the treetops and cool waters flow,
Clouds are white and fleecy, the skies are blue above,
And everywhere about me the air is filled with love.
Come walk in my garden. It's filled with lovely flowers
Blooming in the sunshine, washed with April showers.
It's peaceful in my garden. A hush of happiness
Fills the air around me and brings a quiet rest.

Come walk in my garden; come while the sun is high.
My brightest flower is fading; I fear that it will die.
The winter winds are blowing. The skies are growing dark.
No basking in the sunshine or strolling through the park.
Come walk with me now; hold tight to my hand.
So many things have happened that I don't understand.
My brightest flower has withered. It slowly bowed its head.
I found it there one evening lying cold and dead.

All the flowers are crying the loss of endless years.
The dew upon the roses has turned to bitter tears.
I grope along in darkness. No light shines from above.
Walk softly in my garden, and let me feel your love.
Come walk in my garden. It is no longer light.
The golden rays of sunshine give way to darkest night.
I am walking in the shadows of death and deep despair.
There's danger all around me, and darkness everywhere.

I grope along in silence, searching for God's face.
My heart is filled with anguish, for I long to feel His grace.
I am faced with only quiet when I call on Him in prayer.
I cannot hear an answer, only stillness everywhere.
Come walk in my garden. The flowers are no more.
The path that runs through it is now all grown o'er
With briers and with thistles; It's ugly and bare,
Filled with dark shadows and clouds everywhere.

No bird songs now greet me when I enter the gate.
Just an echo of silence where I pause to wait
For the sound of your voice or the touch of your hand,
But I find only nothing on the path where I stand.
And I know deep inside me I never shall hear
The sound of your footsteps falling soft on my ear,
Nor the sound of your laughter; there's no need to wait.
I'll leave now my garden and close softly the gate.

Another garden lies somewhere beyond my garden wall,
Where darkness never enters, and shadows never fall.
I am walking slowly just behind you on the way.
The garden over yonder is getting nearer every day.
When life's sun within me is a flickering flame,
In the stillness of death I'll whisper your name,
And run swiftly to meet you if you'll pause to wait,
Where the roses are blooming inside Heaven's gate.

Your Grave

You said you didn't want
To be buried, so I said
I'd lay you to rest in a Mausoleum.
But when I looked at that brick wall,
I knew I couldn't put you there.
So I laid you to rest beneath the sky,
Where flowers bloom and birds sing;
Where the sun warms the cold ground,
And there is room for me beside you.
It is quiet now as I stand beside the patch of green
That makes a cover for your bed.
I want to lie beside you, feel your warmth
And the steady beating of your heart.
In the quiet stillness, somehow I know
Someday God will pull back the covers
And tuck me in.

I Miss You

I miss you when the dark
Unwraps a new day
And holds it out to me,
And when a touch of sun
Shines through the dawn
And fills my world with warmth.
I miss you when the night
Folds its arms around the day
And holds it close
Until it fades into memory.
I miss you when the autumn fires
Burn your image in the sky,
And when the frozen white
Rocks my world to sleep.
I miss you when spring
Reflects the dawn of life
And life reflects the memory
Of your death.

A Ghost Town

The store fronts are dirty with cracked, pealing paint.
Broken windows are shrouded with dust and shattered shades.
Signs hang helplessly by a single thread,
Dangling stark and naked as I pass by.
Park benches wait on tree-lined lanes.
Beads of rain cling fast where no one sits.
Brick streets echo past laughter and muted music,
Reflect dead faces and silent voices.

Standing here in the stillness, I feel a part of it.
I remember past years of happiness
When my world was filled with laughter.
When brightly lit stores beckoned to me,
And the streets were filled with people laughing, talking.
Now I see through eyes curtained with reality.
I hear silent voices, and see dead faces.
The park benches are deserted, empty.
Without you my world is a Ghost town.

Winter In My Heart

When I was young and free from care,
Flowers were blooming everywhere,
Birds were singing in the trees,
Gently swaying in the breeze.
It was always springtime in my heart.

The one spring day you came along,
My heart learned to sing love's song.
I loved you so, how could I know
The winter winds would some day blow
And chase the springtime from my heart?

The sun was shining on that day
You said goodbye and went away.
You took the sunshine and the flowers,
The fragrance from the April showers,
And now it's winter in my heart.

I'll never hear the sparrows sing,
Never feel the warmth of spring.
My heart is full of ice and snow;
The sun will never shine I know.
It's winter now forever in my heart.

Who Is She

Who is she who looks at me
From the mirror on my wall?
The face I see is strange to me.
I know her not at all.
Could she be a part of me?
An echo from my past?
Standing there, she can only stare
From my silver looking glass.
Seems to me that she may be
Someone I once have known,
But standing now, she seems somehow
So very much alone.
Is she then a foe or friend?
I do not know at all
The face I see that looks at me
From the mirror on my wall.

Come Walk With Me

Come walk with me; it is midnight now.
All around me is quiet,
But there is no calm in my soul,
Only pain so deep that words won't come.
Prayer is but a tear
Slipping unbidden from my eyes,
Falling softly into the stillness.
There are questions that lurk in the darkness:
Who is this person inside of me?
From where did she come?
Where is she going?
I really don't like her much
Even though I don't know her very well,

And I can't seem to get acquainted with her.
I don't think she is my friend,
And I want the other person back.
She vanished one day with no warning.
Suddenly she just wasn't there.
I search for her everywhere.
I walk in places where she used to walk,
But I can't find her.
I watch the sunset over the western horizon,
Thinking surely I will find her there
Where she loved to be,
But she doesn't watch the sunset anymore.
I walk in crowded places
Where she liked to walk alone.
At times I think I catch a glimpse of her,
But then she disappears,
And I don't know if I really saw her.
I sit still in the darkness

Waiting for the peace that
Used to fill my heart.
But there is no peace,
Only darkness, pain and stillness.
Stillness . . . and nothing.
Is she gone forever?
Will she come back to live
Inside of me again?
Will I wake up some morning
And find her there just as suddenly
As she went away?
I think I know where she has gone.
She is lying in a grave cold and dead,
Lying beside the other part of her.
And that is all right because,
That is where she belongs
With him. I will not disturb her
Even though I miss her so much.

There Is Hope

The days that stretch before me seem so long.
I feel as though I am talking one slow step
After another along an endless journey.
I hear sounds of life somewhere just out of reach,
People laughing, talking, happy in their world.,
But all is still in my world.
There is no laughter here, no sounds of joy.
My world is filled with pain, shattered dreams,
Tears and loneliness . . . horrible loneliness.
Friends reach out to me,
But I turn from their outstretched arms.
I don't want to be touched.
For I am afraid the wall around me will crumble,
And I will crumble with it . . .
Crumble into a thousand shattered pieces
That can never be put together again.
There is something else in my world.
There is hope, like a tiny light in the darkness,
Not bright enough to see where to walk,
Or the path back to the main road,
But it is there, and though it is small, it is burning.
I fix my eyes upon it, and somewhere inside of me
I am glad for its glow.
I know that somehow, if I watch it,
It will lead me out of this maze of darkness
Into the real world again
Where there is laughter and love.

Faith

It is long past midnight, and I sit here alone.
The nights are so long when sleep won't come.
A thousand questions crowd my mind,
Like a flood of muddy waters
Swirling inside my head.
I know you make the final decision, Lord,
In life and death situations,
But I find myself wondering
How it is that one incident can change
The whole course of one's life.
I don't question your wisdom, Lord;
I know you have a reason for the things you do,
But why didn't you give us some warning?
It all happened so suddenly, and I feel cheated,
Because I didn't get to say goodbye.

I don't know who I am now, Lord.
I have tried to find the person I used to be,
But she isn't here. Where has she gone?
Sometimes I think she also died
That hot summer day years ago.
I catch a glimpse of her now and then,
But it is only a fleeting thing;
A flickering light somewhere
In the darkness of bygone days,
And I know she is not really dead,
But hiding somewhere for a while.
Then its weak flame is soon snuffed out
By the swirling, muddy waters inside my head,
And I am not sure anymore
Whether she is dead, or just hiding

Why can't I pick up the pieces of
My broken shattered life?
Why does this horrible hurt consume me so?
Is there a weakness inside of me
That causes me to love so completely
That I exist only in the object of my love?
I am trying hard to understand,
To find some meaning to it all.
But my life seems to be in tiny shattered pieces.
When I pick up one piece, it suddenly breaks
Into a thousand more,
Each one more complex than the other.
I am consumed with it.

I realize that each shattered part of me
Is so broken that there is no way
To fit it with another, no way
To put the pieces together again,
Because they are so damaged
That they don't fit anymore.
It is as though a tornado
Has ripped through my heart
Destroying everything in its path,
Leaving only broken stubble when it is gone.

There is something I need to tell you, Lord.
During all this pain and confusion
I am aware of an amazing fact.
One thing remains untouched.
It is rooted so deeply inside of me
That nothing can destroy it.
It defies the whirlwind,
The muddy waters, the pain.
It cries out in the still dark hours,
"I still believe in you God!
You are somewhere all mixed up
In the shattered pieces of my life,
But You are here, inside of me.
Thank you God for this faith!"

I Lean On Him

It is quiet in my world. There is no laughter here,
Just mostly pain and darkness and sometimes doubt and fear.
Not many people walk here, and oft alone am I.
Nights are filled with darkness, and a heart that wonders why.
I'm faced with uncertainty through I don't understand;
I lift my eyes to heaven and feel Him take my hand.
The future lies before me, a way I cannot see.
I'm content to know I love Him, assured that He loves me.
Whatever He is planning, I'm sure that He knows best.
So in the quiet darkness I lean on Him and rest.

Ode To A Christian Soldier

In a lonely graveyard, a Christian soldier lies.
His armor laid aside, he rests.
His body is a feast for the toothless worms;
His Bible is yellow
And crumbling with age.

The years so swiftly fading into the realm of time,
And memory's candle flickering low,
Cloud the thoughts of yesterday,
While silver threads of nature wait
To hear these words, "Now is the time."

Then he will no longer lie there
Subject to the changing seasons,
For on that day his Captain will lay a healing hand
On his decaying corpse, and new life will flow
Through a resurrected body.

His bible will not be entirely lost, for on that day
He will pick up the crumbled pages
And hand them to His Captain
Who will stamp the words, "Well done"
Upon its cover.

Thank You For The Memories

Thank you for the memories
Of days now long since passed.
When o'er the years of long ago
Time's endless shadows cast.

The moments spent together
Have faded from my view,
But with each shrouded sunset
Comes mystic thoughts of you

That opens up the treasure chest
I've stored within my heart
Of happy times, of by gone days
Before we had to part.

Those happy days are threatened now
By stark reality,
But in the shadowy maze of time
I hold them close to me.

And cherish them each passing day
From dawn till sunset hue,
Knowing that time cannot erase
My memories of you.

Walk Softly Through The Shadows

Walk softly through the shadows
Amid the blue and gray
Where purple fingers gently trace
Embers of the day.
Where mystic hands of white
Spread ashes of the night
Across the milky way.
Walk softly through the shadows.
There's glory hidden there,
And strength is freely given
At the whisper of a prayer.
Where angels from above
Sing their songs of love
To those who travel there.

Walk softly through the shadows.
A little farther on
The gray will blend with golden rays.
The shadows will be gone.
And feelings of distress
Will change to peace and rest
And grace to travel on.
Walk softly through the shadows;
When its mystery fades away
There'll be a golden sunrise
In a land of endless day,
Where a Savior in delight
Flings out rays of light
And wipes the tears away.